Library Lifesavers

Library Lifesavers

A Survival Guide for Stressed Out Librarians

Pamela S. Bacon and Tamora K. Bacon
(a.k.a. The Self-Help Sisters)

LIBRARIES UNLIMITED
An Imprint of ABC-CLIO, LLC

A B C 🔖 C L I O

Santa Barbara, California • Denver, Colorado • Oxford, England

Library of Congress Cataloging-in-Publication Data

Bacon, Pamela S., 1964–
  Library lifesavers : a survival guide for stressed out librarians /
Pamela S. Bacon and Tamora K. Bacon.
    p. cm.
  Includes bibliographical references and index.
  ISBN 978-1-59158-768-2 (acid-free paper)
  1. School libraries—United States. 2. Instructional materials
centers—United States. I. Bacon, Tammy K. II. Title.
  Z675.S3B195 2010
  027.8'0973—dc22   2009039374

ISBN: 978-1-59158-768-2

14 13 12 11 10   1 2 3 4 5

This book is also available on the World Wide Web as an eBook.
Visit http://www.abc-clio.com for details.
Libraries Unlimited
An Imprint of ABC-CLIO, LLC

ABC-CLIO, LLC
130 Cremona Drive, P.O. Box 1911
Santa Barbara, California 93116-1911

This book is printed on acid-free paper ∞

Manufactured in the United States of America

This book is dedicated to our Self-Help Sisters everywhere . . . you know who you are!

CONTENTS

Lifesaver Chapter 1:
Take Action!

Lifesaver Chapter 2:
Hurry No More! "Wait a Minute!"

Lifesaver Chapter 3:
Read All About It! Regain Control!

Lifesaver Chapter 4:
Inspire and Invigorate . . . Yourself and Others

Lifesaver Chapter 5:
View . . . Looking Out After Looking In

Lifesaver Chapter 6:
Excercise . . . Your Mind and Body

LIFESAVER TOOL #	TOOL TITLE	TOOL TYPE
Lifesaver Tool #1	"Job Description Drafting Tool"	Job Description Worksheet
Lifesaver Tool #2	"Annual Report Template"	Annual Report Form
Lifesaver Tool #3	"Presentation Planner"	Presentation Planning Form
Lifesaver Tool #4	"Job Target Tracking Form"	Job Target Worksheet
Lifesaver Tool #5	"What's the Temperature?"	Climate Tips
Lifesaver Tool #6	"Plan on It!"	Weekly Planning Form
Lifesaver Tool #7.1	"Mail Call Tracking Form"	Mail Organizer
Lifesaver Tool #7.2	"Mail Minutes"	Time Tracker Form
Lifesaver Tool #8	"Delegating Dos and Don'ts"	Delegating Form
Lifesaver Tool #9.1	"Shhh! No Talking!"	Problem/Solution Form
Lifesaver Tool #9.2	"Shhh! No Talking!" Sample	Problem/Solution Form (Sample)
Lifesaver Tool #10	"Perfect Versus 'Pretty Good'"	Perfectionism Form
Lifesaver Tool #11	"How Do You Manage It All?"	Time Management Form
Lifesaver Tool #12	"Where Does Your Energy Go?"	Problem/Solution Chart
Lifesaver Tool #13	"Exhaust Your Resources"	Problem/Solution Form
Lifesaver Tool #14.1	"What's Working? What's Not?"	Organization Chart
Lifesaver Tool #14.2	"Chore Chart!"	Time Tracker Form
Lifesaver Tool #15	"No More Monkey Business!"	Weekly Tool Planner
Lifesaver Tool #16	"Ready, Aim, Fire!"	Brainstorming Form
Lifesaver Tool #17	"Be on Your Best Behavior!"	Behavior Contract Form
Lifesaver Tool #18	"Have You Tried 'Dignified?'"	Interview Form
Lifesaver Tool #19	"Teacher Toolbox"	PPL Strategy Form
Lifesaver Tool #20	"Hold on a Minute!"	Getting-To-Know-You Form
Lifesaver Tool #20.1	"Invigorate!" Example #1	Tried It-Tam
Lifesaver Tool #20.2	"Invigorate!" Example #2	Tried It-Pam
Lifesaver Tool #21.1	"Get It 'Booked!'"	Book Club Planning Sheet
Lifesaver Tool #21.2	"Get It 'Booked!'" Example	Tried It Tribute-Weliever
Lifesaver Tool #22	"Online-Only Book Club Rating Form"	Book Rating Form
Lifesaver Tool #23	"Well? Why Not?"	Wellness Survey
Lifesaver Tool #24	"Food Fun Days!"	Food Day Form
Lifesaver Tool #25	"You're My Inspiration!"	Inspirational Record
Lifesaver Tool #26	"View Your Future!"	Action Planning Sheet

LIFESAVER TOOL #	TOOL TITLE	TOOL TYPE
Lifesaver Tool #27.1	"Candid Camera: View Your Present"	Candid Camera Page
Lifesaver Tool #27.2	"Candid Camera: View Your Present" Example	Tried It Tribute-Witty
Lifesaver Tool #28	"Your Passionate Place"	Scrapbook Page
Lifesaver Tool #29	"Your Professional View"	Press Release Template
Lifesaver Tool #30	"Present and Future Views"	Snapshot Goal Form
Lifesaver Tool #31	"You've Got to Move It, Move It!"	Music Graphic Organizer
Lifesaver Tool #32	" 'Before and After' Yoga Reflection Sheet"	Yoga Reflection Sheet
Lifesaver Tool #33	"Think the Worst!"	Think Graphic Organizer #1
Lifesaver Tool #34.1	"Think the Best!"	Think Graphic Organizer #2
Lifesaver Tool #34.2	"Think the Best!" Example	Tried It Tribute-Janice
Lifesaver Tool #35.1	"Make It Work . . . Out!"	Workout Weekly Planner
Lifesaver Tool #35.2	"Rest Your Mind . . . and Body"	Nap Scheduler/Planner

INTRODUCTION

We may be identical twins, but our ideas are anything but. We've written this book for real teachers and librarians (aren't they one and the same?) who are struggling to survive . . . and thrive . . . in the classroom and media center. With two points of view, you'll find the tone to be sometimes argumentative (after all, Tam has been an administrator!), sometimes bantering, but always positive! You'll find a conversational, upbeat tone—whether you choose to read the book cover-to-cover with activities completed in sequential order (Tam's preference) or in random order on a whim (Pam's pick). Each section begins with a real-life question followed by practical advice and hands-on activities to help librarian-teachers renew, reflect, and, ultimately, rejoice! We know that while teaching can be the most rewarding, ful- filling career, it can also be the most stressful. Trying to juggle the needs of students, parents, and administrators is difficult and can easily lead to burnout. That's where this book comes in. Having been there, done that . . . and still doing it . . . we want to motivate other educators to be the best they can be—both in and out of the library and classroom!

Here's What You'll Find . . .

Lifesavers #1 through #35
Talk   Q and A (followed by lively discussion)
Test   Quick questionnaire or survey to determine your strengths
Tips   Advice from the trenches
Tools   Reproducible Hands-On Activities
Talk About It!   Counselor's Corner Conversations (advice and insight
                              featuring Becky Greenlee, a licensed school counselor)
Think and Reflect   Journal Prompts

Appendices
Trips   Internet links to enhance your reading experience

OUTLINE

Take action

- "Get It Together!"

  Find out how you can reduce stress while getting the job done. This chapter focuses on everything from action plans to job descriptions so you can "get it together" both personally and professionally!

Hurry no more

- "Wait a Minute!"

  Learn how slowing down can help you be more productive and actually get more done in a fast-paced library through the help of effective time-management strategies and helpful organizers.

Read . . . reflect, and refocus

- "Read All About It!"

  As librarians, we know all about the power of books. You'll want to check out our top ten picks for reflection and renewal.

Invigorate . . . yourself and others

- "How Does She Do It?"

  That's what others will be saying when they see the energy and enthusiasm you'll have after trying out the inspiring activities in this chapter.

View . . . look out after looking in

- "Take a Picture . . . It Lasts Longer!"

  Discover your personal vision as you look out from under your work-buried desk and "see" how your professional and personal life can really be!

Exercise . . . your mind and body

- "Make It Work . . . Out!"

  Find out how exercising the body can keep you from losing your mind!

Chapter 1

Take Action!

Take Action!

Talk

Q. I am a busy librarian who travels between schools. In addition, I keep getting more and more added to my already packed job description! What can I do to take action and finally get my head above water?

—Lighten-My-Load Librarian

As an administrator, I worked closely with my librarian—when I could find her! She was constantly on the go! I know that she would have appreciated the "Take Action" ideas in this chapter.

Tam

Well, sometimes finding an administrator can be the hard part. After trying the lifesavers in this chapter, we may never need an administrator (no offense!).

Pam

Take the Test!

1-Requires Immediate Action	2-Requires Future Action	3-Requires No Action at This Time

Directions: Place a number (from the chart above) beside each question indicating the status needed for each item.

1. _____ My job description is updated, clear, and reflects current roles and responsibilities (JOB DESCRIPTION).

2. _____ I complete an annual report each year that accurately portrays the strengths and concerns of the program (ANNUAL REPORT).

3. _____ I have made staffing needs known to my principal, have documented my staffing issues, and have provided relevant data (STAFFING and PR).

4. _____ When staffing conflicts and/or issues arise, I have a communication plan in place to support the staff member, document the issue of concern, and encourage future improvement (JOB TARGETS and STAFF EVALUATION).

5. _____ My discipline plan is effective and the overall climate of the media center is positive and welcoming (DISCIPLINE).

Tam's To-Do

LIFESAVER #1: What exactly am I supposed to do? Defining roles and responsibilities.

One of the challenges that we found in our corporation was the changing role of the library media specialist! In fact, we weren't even sure exactly what the official title was—librarian, media specialist, library media specialist, etc. We found, like most corporations, there was not an updated job description that truly encompassed the additional job responsibilities and roles that had been added since her original hire. We encourage you to review the following Web site to research the many different job descriptions and standards associated with the invaluable and changing role of the "new and improved" library media specialist: http://www.sldirectory.com/libsf/resf/evaluate.html#jobs.

TIPS:

- Review and research the varied roles and responsibilities in a variety of job descriptions.

- Meet with your administrator(s) to determine their vision for your position and what their specific priorities are for your building—it may be completely different from your perception.

- Request a copy of any existing job descriptions from your personnel director.

- Clearly define to whom you are responsible to report, who evaluates you, and additional information related to the nature and scope of your position.

- Take some time to reflect on your hopes, dreams, and wishes for your role and position. Don't be afraid to "think outside the circulation desk."

- Use Lifesaver Tool #1 to begin drafting your revised document.

- Provide copies of the finalized report to your administration.

- Request a review of these along with your annual report each year.

- Consider creating and/or updating job descriptions for your library assistants—if you are lucky enough to have them!

Job Description Drafting Tool

Position Title:

Reports To:

Evaluation Process:

Roles and Responsibilities:

   A. Information Specialist:

       Performance Expectations:

       Knowledge Needed:

       Disposition:

   B. Instructional Leadership:

       Performance Expectations:

       Knowledge Needed:

       Disposition:

   C. Teaching Responsibilities:

       Performance Expectations:

       Knowledge Needed:

       Disposition:

       Questions/Clarifications Needed:

Lifesaver Tool #1

Pam's To-Do

LIFESAVER #2: You're on Report!

Although an annual report is not listed in my job responsibilities, it is one of my top priorities at the end of each year. Not only does it provide my administration with valuable information, it is a way to get closure and pat myself on the back each May! In addition, I use this great tool as a basis for determining strengths and weaknesses and for future goal setting. You will "sink" into this in the next chapter! Check this out: http://www.sldirectory. com/libsf/resf/studies.html#annual.

TIPS:

- Review the examples and suggestions at the link above.

- Be proactive! Plan ahead using Lifesaver Tool #2 to jot down your notes throughout the year so that you won't have to scramble at the last minute.

- Start a folder on your desk and computer desktop for data collection.

- Use student interviews to provide interesting comments on key areas of your program. Take pictures of those students with their latest read for the report—pictures make the comments "real" with higher-ups, who can see a student's face along with the comment.

- Survey your staff! Include their valuable insights in your report.

- Remember that a picture is worth a thousand words! Keep a digital camera handy for getting snapshots of your successful activities and programs throughout the year.

- Request a meeting with your administration to discuss touchy areas prior to presenting the report to stakeholders.

Annual Report Template

- Artifacts: Which artifacts do I want to keep?
  Consider student work samples, digital pictures, video clips, PowerPoint presentations, news releases, survey samples, interview responses, etc.

- Data, data, data! Which pieces of data will be the most valuable to include? Consider circulation reports, collection-development information, co-teaching projects, student achievement data, etc.

- How can I hook the audience? Consider what theme might catch the attention of the reader. Collect cartoons, visuals, and artifacts throughout the year for use in your report.

- Strengths/concerns: After analyzing the data, determine your program strengths and areas of concern. Don't be afraid to "toot your own horn"—you have worked hard and deserve recognition! For areas of concern, have some goals for problem solving in mind and list these in your report.

- Needs for next year and future programming: This is a time to request in writing what you might have been saying throughout the year. Be specific and direct in your approach.

- End on a positive! The squeaky wheel gets the grease, but not the funding!

Lifesaver Tool #2

Tam's To-Do

LIFESAVER #3: Show Me the Money!

I agree that a strong annual report is a very important part of raising awareness and creating positive relations for your program. With today's limited budgets and cuts in staffing, it is critical to "sell your program." If you are hoping to create additional staffing (or keep what you currently have), this section will benefit you. Review the web link below for a great example of a professional presentation that will help your administrators begin to dig deep into their pockets to find funding sources! These sites are truly some of the best examples we've seen. Check them out:

> http://www.resa.net/services/grants/resources/grantproposaltemplate/
> http://www.doug-johnson.com/dougwri/when-your-job-is-on-the-line.html

TIPS:

- Review outstanding proposals from other schools within or outside of your school corporation.

- Network with peers who have been successful in securing funding for staffing in their schools.

- Consider places that you could cut back in your budget in order to assist with funding for additional staff.

- Be creative! Technology funds are often available and can be used for library assistant funds if their job descriptions match (or can be tweaked to match) the technology goals for your corporation.

- Use Lifesaver Tool #3 to draft your presentation.

- Include key parts of your successes from your annual report, as well as student achievement data as appropriate.

- Collaborate with peers and school staff in brainstorming ideas and as an audience for practicing your presentation.

- When presenting to administration and/or school board members, be sure to dress professionally and, whenever possible, include students!

Presentation Planner

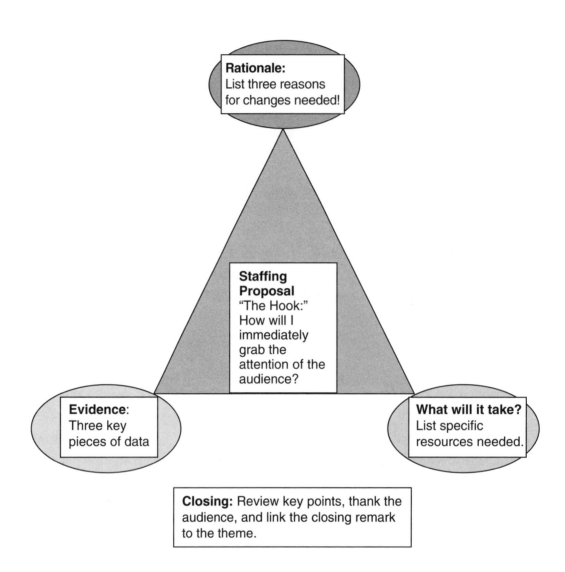

Pam's To-Do

LIFESAVER #4: Job Targets—When It Must Be Said!

One of the most difficult tasks for me is working with support staff on job targets. When you work closely with someone day in and day out, the last thing you want to have to do is discuss and document their areas of weakness. In the case of an insubordinate worker, it can create an extremely uncomfortable situation. However, I have found that sometimes it is necessary to "go there" in order to protect your program (and your students)! The following site can assist you: http://office.microsoft.com/en-us/templates/TC060889521033.aspx.

TIPS:

- Review the link above and the variety of templates available for documenting job targets.

- Be as objective as possible. Let your data speak for itself.

- Seek a win/win situation when at all possible. Let your assistant know that you want to provide him/her with the necessary support needed to improve.

- Be honest. This problem won't be resolved without open and honest communication.

- Put it on paper! If you are like me, my communication in writing can be much stronger than my verbal communication.

- Document, document, document—the good, the bad, and "the ugly!"

- Brainstorm solutions with your administrator—does your assistant have strengths that could allow him/her to be transferred into another role? Are these concerns documented from year's past? You will need administrative support if improvement does not occur and action needs to be taken.

- Use Lifesaver Tool #4 to document needed job targets and his/her performance.

- Set a weekly meeting time to review and discuss progress or concerns on a regular basis.

Job Target Tracking Form

Name_____

Position_____

Date Initiated_____

Job Target Goals:
(List up to three)

Training/Support Action Plan:
(List the training and support that you will provide as well as self-development expectations such as readings, peer observations, etc.)

Documentation of Areas of Improvement or Concerns During Review Period:

Specific Dates for Implementation: _____

Date for Next Job Target Review: _____

Supervisor's Signature: _____

Additional Comments:

Lifesaver Tool #4

Our To-Do

LIFESAVER #5: Survival Strategies from the Trenches—When the Library Feels
Like a "War Zone!"

No matter what your role in education—administration, librarian, teacher, interventionist, or special area teacher—discipline problems are the number one stressor! We both agree that in order to take back your library, you need strategies that work. Check out these tips: http://www.iidc.indiana.edu/CELL/docs/Mental-Set.pdf.

TIPS:

- Before you can take care of anyone else, you need to take care of yourself. Be sure that you are approaching your job with the right mental attitude.

- Read through the strategies throughout this book on creating a balanced life and dealing with stress.

- Review your current policies and procedures for discipline. Are they up to date? Can they be enforced? Are they posted?

- Consider meeting with a student group to discuss the climate, rules, and procedures.

- Enlist students in helping you to problem-solve steps for improvement.

- Work with your administrator and/or counselor to create individual student behavior plans for consistently out-of-control students.

- Be creative! What teacher could you partner with to use the time-out strategy? Is a resource teacher available for special education students to assist with redirection?

- Consider a "Three Strikes You're Out!" rule for misbehaving students at the junior high or high school level. If a student gets three strikes, he/she can't come back into the media center for thirty days.

- Think win/win! Be willing to show some flexibility in order to get what you both want.

- Reluctant to discipline? Read *Reluctant Disciplinarian* by Gary Rubinstein (Cottonwood Press, 1999). This classroom-management book is full of helpful advice from a former "softy!"

- Review and research the Positive School Behavior (PBS) program.

  Consider implementing it in your school. This program involves specifically teaching the behaviors that you expect by consistently modeling procedures and routines. Incentives and positive reinforcement are built into the program.

- Refer to Lifesaver Tool #5 for positive climate pointers.

What's the Temperature?

C—Calmly and respectfully state your expectations.

L—Lecturing never works—try brainstorming a new solution. Offer limited choices when possible.

I—Implement your plan. Be fair and consistent. Be proactive.

M—Model the expected behavior. Teach the procedures and demonstrate the process. (Even when they should know it!)

A—Avoid power struggles—plan to ignore the problem behavior if it isn't dangerous to others.

T—Talk to the problem student in private whenever possible.

E—Expect the best! Begin each day with a fresh start.

Lifesaver Tool #5

TALK ABOUT IT: COUNSELOR'S CORNER

We all know too well that change can be very scary! Sometimes in education, it seems that the only thing we can truly count on is more change. I want to encourage you to start small when taking on a new action plan. Try changing one bad habit and replacing it with a positive action. (For me, one example was setting my alarm ten minutes earlier each day in order to spend that time doing something positive for myself. I tend to meet everyone's needs before my own—sound familiar?) Remember that it only takes three weeks for a new habit to be developed and for it to become part of your new routine. You can do it!

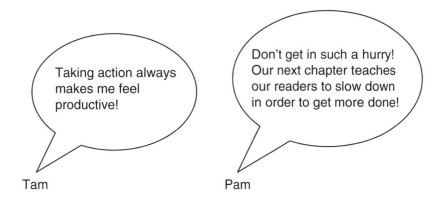

Think and Reflect: Journal Prompt

Only you can take the actions necessary to make positive changes in your life, both personally and professionally.

Determine areas in which you feel that you need to take more control—or less.
Journal your personal thoughts and reflections now.

Chapter 2

Hurry No More! "Wait a Minute!"

Hurry No More!
"Wait a Minute!"

Talk

Q. Even though I'm working longer and longer hours, I find myself getting less done. Everyone else in the building is gone, and I find myself feeling bogged down. What can I do to be more productive?

—Late-Again Librarian

As a previous administrator, I find action plans are the best way to save time and energy. Acting now will allow you extra time for renewal later. Act now!

Tam

What's the hurry? Too many times we rush around checking off our to-do lists and end up getting less done, not more. When you're tired and stressed, you can't be productive. My advice? Do nothing!

Pam

Take the Test!

ARE YOU A PROCRASTINATOR? FIND OUT NOW!		
1. I always get work turned in by the deadline.		
Rarely ☹	Sometimes	Usually ☺
2. I keep a to-do list and refer to it regularly.		
Rarely ☹	Sometimes	Usually ☺
3. I never put off planning for an upcoming project.		
Rarely ☹	Sometimes	Usually ☺
4. Teachers and administrators can count on me to follow through.		
Rarely ☹	Sometimes	Usually ☺
5. I break large projects into small chunks to avoid feeling overwhelmed.		
Rarely ☹	Sometimes	Usually ☺

Scoring guide: The goal is to have all "usually" answers. This reflective test can be used often as a vision checkup. Use the questions you answered "rarely" or "sometimes" as an action plan to improve how often you procrastinate. Don't put it off—do it now!

Tam's To-Do

LIFESAVER #6: Act Now . . . or Forever Hold Your To-Do List!

Although some people (i.e., Pam) might feel that I am an "over-planner," I have always prided myself as being someone with strong time-management and organizational skills. In my experience as an administrator and literacy coach, I find that a well-thought-out plan of action is the key to making the most of my personal and professional time.

TIPS:

- Use Lifesaver Tool #6 to create a weekly action plan consisting of three prioritized goals.

- Take time to reflect on the priority of your goals—some can be placed on next week's action plan, while some must remain urgent in priority.

- Break the goal down into three key actions—be specific.

- Include a target date and document your completion date(s).

- Consider what items might be able to be delegated—see more about this in Lifesaver Tool #8.

- Take time to celebrate your weekly accomplishments!

- Don't spend time "beating yourself up" over items not completed.

- Add incomplete goals to the following week's action plan as appropriate.

- Reflect on how effective and productive you were this week by utilizing a specific action plan.

"Plan on It!"
Action Plan Sheet—Weekly

Goal 1: _____

       Action Steps: Target Date/Completed

       A: _____

       B: _____

       C: _____

Comments/Next Steps:

Goal 2: _____

       Action Steps: Target Date/Completed

       A: _____

       B: _____

       C: _____

Comments/Next Steps:

Goal 3: _____

       Action Steps: Target Date/Completed

       A: _____

       B: _____

       C: _____

Comments/Next Steps:

Rate Myself: Did I "hurry no more" and take action this week?

Yes—Much improved   Somewhat—Better   No—Don't even go there!

Lifesaver Tool #6

Pam's To-Do

LIFESAVER #7: Mail Call . . . Dos and Don'ts of the Top Three "Mails" in Our Lives!

For this lifesaver, I really, really wanted to leave the page blank. I thought a blank page with the words "Do Nothing!" would really make a statement and prove to my audience that I truly do believe in this philosophy. However, Tam wouldn't let me (humpff!). After a brief argument, she won, so here goes!

Because voice mail, e-mail, and snail mail are truly some of the biggest tasks a media specialist tackles on a daily basis, I made up a simple list of dos and don'ts. "Do" take some time to read it, but just remember: "Don't" do anything when you're too tired and frustrated . . . you'll just make mistakes that will end up costing you more time in the long run. Lifesaver Tool #7.1 is a tool to help you control the mails in your life (if only it was that easy!); Lifesaver Tool #7.2 is a log to help you keep track of mail to-dos.

TIPS FOR VOICE MAIL:

- Do request a phone with a voice mail light.

- Don't waste time checking the phone when there are no voice mails in your in-box.

- Do log all voice mails (see Lifesaver Tool #7.1) to follow up on later . . . if no immediate action is needed.

- Don't act immediately by returning a call that doesn't require immediate attention.

- Do set your phone to voice mail when you have a deadline looming.

- Don't be distracted by a ringing telephone when you are under deadline pressure.

- Do update your voice mail regularly . . . a "welcome back" greeting in December is embarrassing!

- Don't forget to check your voice mails!

- Do put a Post-it note on your calendar each month to remind you to update your voice mail.

- Don't put too much information on your voice mail. Just provide the basics for busy callers!

TIPS FOR SNAIL MAIL:

- Do set up an organization system with three bins. Label the bins "To Do Now," "To Do Later," and "To Discard." Note: Discard might mean trashing or giving to someone else who could use it!

- Don't use the bin system as a multipurpose area. By delegating the bins strictly for snail mail, you'll stay more organized, and your time won't be "trashed!"

- Do assign a time to sort through mail daily. Librarians get so much mail that mail call is a big part of our jobs!

- Don't get behind on mail. If you must be out of the office, delegate the task to a trained assistant so you won't come back to an overflowing mailbox and piled-high in-box.

- Do deal with each piece of mail immediately. By taking no action on an item and/or shuffling the piece two or three times, you've wasted valuable time—and still haven't dealt with the item in question.

- Don't procrastinate on items . . . deal with them immediately. Be honest! If you don't have time to follow up on something, admit it and move on. Perhaps pass the item to someone who can use it.

- Do ask an assistant to call and remove you from mailing lists for catalogs you don't need. You don't need to waste the time—and you can save someone else's time and money by being taken off the list. Go green and put a stop to mailbox clutter.

- Don't ignore unwanted junk mail. It will just pile up!

- Do throw away immediately something someone else has. When it doubt, throw it out!

- Don't keep catalogs or mail that you can get from someone else. In terms of brain space and office space, it's best to let it go!

TIPS FOR E-MAIL:

- Do set a time daily to check e-mail. Because e-mail can be addictive, setting a limit to once or twice a day (the beginning of the day and the end of the day) can save you time.

- Don't get addicted to your e-mail!

- Do set up file folders in your e-mail for organization. You can use categories similar to your snail mail ("To Do Now," "To Do Later," and "To Discard"). You can also set up categories by subject. My folders, for example, are "School," "Personal," "Writing," and "Family." Sometimes you don't want a cluttered in-box, but want to keep an e-mail. Folders allow you to easily access these items when YOU want to . . . not when a blinking e-mail light tells you to!

- Don't keep all your e-mail in your in-box. It's bad karma and makes you disorganized and overwhelmed to see 374 e-mails staring back at you!

- Do change your e-mail view to sender if you want to quickly find an e-mail from a specific person.

- Don't forget to change your view back when you are done so that the most current e-mails are on top.

- Do send personal e-mails to your home e-mail address. Many times, personal e-mails can be dealt with later anyway.

- Don't write anything inappropriate (even jokes). School accounts are public domain and can be legally checked by anyone at any time (i.e., newspapers). You wouldn't want to be called in on the carpet for passing on a funny joke . . . especially one about your principal!

- Do delete forwards. Who has the time? (Except for our retired Mom . . . sorry!)

- Don't print out e-mails that you could easily put in a folder. Go green . . . and paperless!

MAIL CALL TRACKING FORM

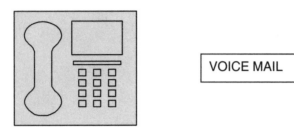

VOICE MAIL

DATE	MESSAGE FROM	NUMBER	ACTION NEEDED	TASK COMPLETED

SNAIL MAIL

DATE	MESSAGE FROM	ADDRESS	ACTION NEEDED	TASK COMPLETED

Lifesaver Tool #7.1

E-MAIL

DATE	MESSAGE FROM	NUMBER	ACTION NEEDED	TASK COMPLETED

Lifesaver Tool #7.1

From *Library Lifesavers: A Survival Guide for Stressed Out Librarians* by Pamela S. Bacon and Tamora K. Bacon. Santa Barbara, CA: Libraries Unlimited. Copyright © 2010.

"MAIL MINUTES!"
MAIL CALL TIME TRACKER

<u>Directions</u>: Choose one day to track your mail to see how much time you spend on a daily basis on these never-ending tasks. Make a tally in the box below every time you deal with a voice mail, snail mail, or e-mail. Total up the number of tally marks. Then read the dos and don'ts in Lifesaver #7. After practicing the dos and don'ts for a few days, use the time-tracker tool again to see if you've saved valuable time!

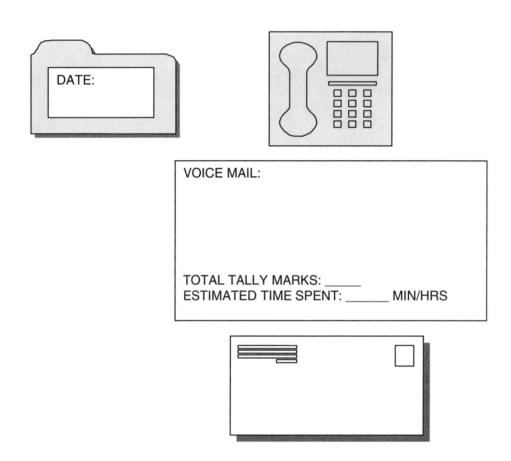

DATE:

VOICE MAIL:

TOTAL TALLY MARKS: _____
ESTIMATED TIME SPENT: _____ MIN/HRS

Lifesaver Tool #7.2

SNAIL MAIL:

TOTAL TALLY MARKS: _____
ESTIMATED TIME SPENT: _____ MIN/HRS

E-MAIL:

TOTAL TALLY MARKS: _____
ESTIMATED TIME SPENT: _____ MIN/HRS

Lifesaver Tool #7.2

From *Library Lifesavers: A Survival Guide for Stressed Out Librarians* by Pamela S. Bacon
and Tamora K. Bacon. Santa Barbara, CA: Libraries Unlimited. Copyright © 2010.

Tam's To-Do

LIFESAVER #8: Don't Wait—Delegate!

I know that Pam often likes to work in solitude so that she can really focus on her projects without interruptions. I, however, have always appreciated a team approach to projects and goal setting. My husband often jokes that whenever we work on a project together, he can tell I have been an "administrator" because of the way I like to delegate tasks. Of course, I assure him that I only delegate to those whom I can trust and respect to get the job done!

Delegating can be a great way to help another team member build his or her skills under your guidance and direction. Don't fall into the "if you need a job done right, do it yourself" trap! Find a coworker whom you trust and who you can mentor to assist you. By taking time now to train them, you will save a lot of time for yourself in the future, as well as build personal and professional friendships. One of the administrators in our district has a motto posted in her building that states, "Every adult is responsible for the success of every other adult." This type of team approach is powerful and helps to create a sense of community and synergy in the school, workplace, and/or media center.

TIPS:

- Use Lifesaver Tool #8 to review the key points of delegation. List tasks, time lines, and people responsible on the chart.

- Include time lines and checkpoints on your weekly action plan so that you can fully support and keep up-to-date on project status.

- Keep a copy of the delegation chart in your file for future reflection.

- Don't get discouraged if your early efforts are not successful—learning to delegate is a process.

- Remember that it is sometimes necessary to "just say no" to a project if you are overly committed.

- Prioritize time to celebrate the successful completion to projects. Reward your team with a special activity or recognition ceremony.

- Try your best not to be a perfectionist—see more information in Lifesaver #10 (forthcoming).

- Remember to offer to help another coworker with a task—by volunteering to take on one of their tasks, the colleague will be an even stronger team member for you in the future.

Delegating Dos and Don'ts: The "Why" and the "How"

W—When you are overwhelmed!

H—Hurry no more! Delegating frees you to focus on your priority goals.

Y—You help build skills of your co-workers and staff members.

H—Handle your biggest action plan items and delegate the others.

O—Offer support, guidance, and realistic time lines to your team.

W—Who is the best person for each task? Determine who can support you and is willing to help.

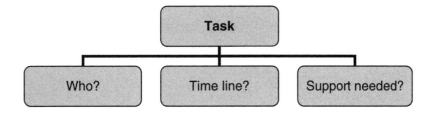

Lifesaver Tool #8

Pam's To-Do

LIFESAVER #9: Put a Lock on It . . . Avoid Time-Takers and Interruptions!

We all have times when the last thing we need is another interruption, especially from a talker (like Tam). There are times when we need to be social and network, but there are other times when we need to avoid interruptions and get 'er done! As a people pleaser, I know personally how difficult this can be. You may feel rude at first when you put up the "Do Not Disturb" sign, but most people will understand when you explain it to them later over a cup of coffee that you actually have time to drink!

TIPS:

- Use Lifesaver Tool #9.1 to track your time-takers and interruptions.

- Reflect on what you can control . . . and what you can't change.

- Use a problem-solution approach to brainstorm possible options for dealing with those frequent time-takers. (See a tried-and-true sample on Lifesaver Tool #9.2.)

- Try many options and/or solutions before throwing in the timer!

- Talk privately to colleagues who are frequent offenders. Chances are, they may not realize how much time you are losing when they come in.

- Be prepared to feel guilty when you put yourself first.

- Be honest and up front. Let people know your new schedule builds in some closed-door time.

Shhh! No Talking . . . Please Don't Interrupt!

Problem	Solution

Lifesaver Tool #9.1

Shhh! No Talking . . . Please Don't Interrupt!

Problem	Solution
While planning for the day and reviewing my action plan, a teacher stops to talk about her weekend—T.	Set up a lunch meeting with the teacher to get caught up and enjoy a nice chat without giving up valuable planning time.
While on prep period, a former favorite student comes in to visit while in study hall—P.	After checking to make sure they have a legit pass, say hi to the student and then tell them you have a meeting or need to use the restroom. Most students won't wait around for you!
Coworker asks you to cover her hall duty—T.	You offer to cover the duty, but ask her to trade you for one of yours—although it requires a schedule change, planning time is not lost.
A teacher who comes into your office to schedule library time gets comfy and doesn't appear to be leaving anytime soon—P.	Make any excuse to politely leave the room. Post your Do Not Disturb sign upon returning.
Someone stops you in the hall to chat—T and P.	Invite them to walk with you to your destination.

Lifesaver Tool #9.2

Our To-Do

LIFESAVER #10: Close Enough to Perfect!

It is no surprise to anyone who knows us well that we can both be quite perfectionistic and people pleasing. This is something that we have to constantly work on! Of course, like most busy media specialists and teachers, it is the most difficult when we are under high stress or multiple work deadlines. We hope that these tips will help others realize that sometimes "good enough" IS perfect!

TIPS:

- Use Lifesaver Tool #10 to reflect on the difference between being "perfect" and accepting something that is "pretty good!"

- Use your weekly action plan to rate your projects on a scale of 1 to 5, with 1 being low priority and 5 being high priority on the "perfect" scale. Plan your time accordingly.

- Find peers and coworkers to assist you with providing objective feedback on tasks and projects to determine when it is "good enough!"

- Remember that we often don't see clearly when we are tired or stressed—there are times when going home and getting a good night's sleep will allow you a better perspective on your projects and tasks.

- Remember that "practice makes perfect" isn't necessarily true—it will take practice to break the perfectionism cycle, but it is important!

- Reach out to help others if you see them caught in this trap—it is often hard to delegate when you are a perfectionist.

Perfect Versus "Pretty Good!"

G—Good time-management guidelines are followed! The time you allotted for the project closely equals the amount of actual time expended.

O—Other coworkers feel that the project is well done and meets the goal.

O—"Open-mindedness"—try to look at the project from an objective viewpoint.

D—Document the strengths and concerns of the project. Note the little things that bother you and how you might avoid them in future projects. Celebrate your ability to let go of your perfectionism in order to more fully appreciate the present!

Project Checklist

Project	Date	Perfect/Pretty Good

Lifesaver Tool #10

TALK ABOUT IT: COUNSELOR'S CORNER

Even as a counselor, I am no stranger to challenges with time management. As an adult, I struggle with ADHD tendencies and find that I have to work very hard to stay focused and on task. As a social person, I find this to be difficult! For me, it helps to write down my top three goals for the day and then prioritize them. (Some people find it helpful to color code their to-do lists to determine their priorities.) It is important to find what works best for you personally. I encourage you to celebrate your accomplishments and provide yourself with positive reinforcement—you deserve it!

Let's get this chapter done, Pam. I've already checked this one off my list!

Tam

Wait a minute! You always seem to be in such a hurry. Why not take some time now to relax and read a great book? Check out the next chapter!

Pam

Think and Reflect: Journal Prompt

Viewing yourself differently will only emerge from a place deep within.

Go to that deep place and reflect upon the view of yourself that you have after reading and reflecting on this chapter.

Chapter 3

Read All About It!
Regain Control!

Read All About It! Regain Control!

Talk

Q. I often feel that I'm spinning my wheels. As soon as I get one thing finished, I find three more things added to my to-do list. With constant discipline interruptions, I don't get anything done. What resources can I use immediately for help?

—Losing-It Librarian

We understand how you feel! With more and more demands, strong time-management skills become more important than ever. Take some "time" to read and reflect on the strategies listed in this chapter so that you are managing the clock, rather than it managing you!

Tam

Now, "wait a minute!" Don't forget that some of these books will save you time and energy—in fact, they help make every "minute" count!

Pam

What would a book for librarians be without a chapter full of "must-reads?" As Tam and I were doing research for our book, we found that the two biggest traps for many librarians were related to either time management or stress from discipline issues. In this chapter, you will find our top ten recommendations for your personal and professional libraries! The following book talks will encourage you to "check it out!"

Test

Got a Minute? Time Management

1. My task list is usually up-to-date and reflects productivity.

Rarely ☹	Sometimes	Usually ☺

2. Overall, I feel that I manage my time well.

Rarely ☹	Sometimes	Usually ☺

3. I usually have closure to several projects and tasks at the end of the day.

Rarely ☹	Sometimes	Usually ☺

4. I often feel positive (rather than overwhelmed) in my work space.

Rarely ☹	Sometimes	Usually ☺

5. Others view me as organized, efficient, and creative.

Rarely ☹	Sometimes	Usually ☺

Got a Minute? Discipline

6. Discipline issues take up the majority of my day.

Rarely ☹	Sometimes	Usually ☺

7. Overall, I feel my discipline strategies are effective.

Rarely ☹	Sometimes	Usually ☺

8. I feel that my library has a positive climate and is student centered.

Rarely ☹	Sometimes	Usually ☺

9. I have many positive relationships with students and have established an atmosphere of mutual respect.

Rarely ☹	Sometimes	Usually ☺

10. I have proactive strategies for dealing with out-of-control students.

Rarely ☹	Sometimes	Usually ☺

Scoring guide: The goal is to have all "usually" answers. This status check can be used regularly for time management and discipline checks . . . whenever you have a "minute!"

Pam's To-Do

LIFESAVER #11: How Do You Manage It All?

Recommended Read: *Time Management for Unmanageable People* by Ann McGee-Cooper.

Are you a "closet creative type" but constantly feel disorganized? I first read this book when I was changing positions. After five years as a classroom teacher, I was hired as an assistant principal for my district. I was taken by surprise when I was selected over other applicants with more experience. I began reading everything I could find on time management and leadership. This book has resonated with me throughout my career. I encourage you to keep a copy and re-read it at different stages of your career. As librarians, you will find the strategies invaluable for those times when you feel out of control and it seems like you can't get anything done!

TIPS:

- Don't mistake a perfectly organized work area as a sign of efficiency.

- Constant "hurrying" can make you less creative and therefore less productive.

- View some unplanned interruptions as a positive.

- Find your own time-management system—don't feel that you have to be confined to someone else's packaged program.

- Have fun with your calendar and schedule—make it yours with your own creative flair!

- Take time for play!

- Find out what your time traps are and make a plan to take control of them.

- Take time to celebrate your accomplishments—you deserve it!

- Puzzled by where your time goes? Use Lifesaver Tool #11 to figure it out!

How Do You Manage It All?

If you had more time, what would you do with it? Motivate yourself by listing your answers on the puzzle pieces below. Celebrate and check them off after implementing the strategies from this book! Fill your office wall with pieces of your success so you're not puzzled about how successful you really are!

Lifesaver Tool #11

Pam's To-Do

LIFESAVER #12: No Time? Take Time!

Recommended Read: *Take Time for Your Life* by Cheryl Richardson.

Do you want to regain control and start making the right decisions to get your work (and personal) life back on track? If so, life coach Cheryl Richardson's seven steps can inspire you to take back the life you want. Step up to a new life using these practical tips.

TIPS:

- Step 1: Learn to put yourself at the top of your to-do list. It's not selfish to be selfish!

- Step 2: Learn to be proactive—not reactive—when managing your schedule.

- Step 3: Learn to eliminate time-takers and energy zappers!

- Step 4: Learn to manage your money and save your sanity!

- Step 5: Learn ways to have healthy energy and rid yourself of unhealthy fuels like caffeine, anger, and other destructive forces.

- Step 6: No librarian is an island. Learn to surround yourself with supportive, positive work relationships.

- Step 7: Learn to connect with your spiritual side and find ways to be renewed and at peace at work.

- Don't let your time go down the drain! Use Lifesaver Tool #12 to help.

WHERE DOES YOUR ENERGY GO?

<u>Directions</u>: Determine your biggest drain. Why is it a problem? What might be a solution? Did the results change after trying the solution? Good luck!

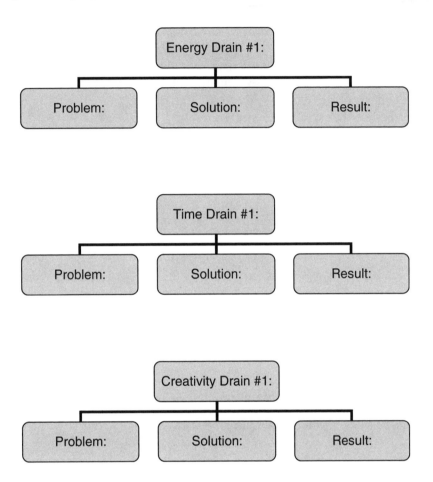

Lifesaver Tool #12

Tam's To-Do

LIFESAVER #13: "Exhaust" All Your Resources

Recommended Read: *You Don't Have To Go Home from Work Exhausted* by Ann McGee-Cooper.

I was hooked on this book when I read the title! "That's me!" I thought—and perhaps you can relate. Ann McGee-Cooper recommends the concept of "Creative Energy Engineering" to take control of your time—and your life. Her writing style is upbeat and creative, which is why both of her books fell in my top ten!

TIPS:

- Don't be afraid to take some risks—be open to some new ways of thinking!

- Remember that if we keep doing things the same way, we will get the same results.

- Take the self-assessment to find your goal areas . . . then use Lifesaver Tool #13 to turn your time around.

- Continue seeking ways to incorporate fun and play into your busy day.

- Take mini joy breaks.

- Study the brain research related to time management. Don't get into negative self-talk if you aren't a type A left-brainer!

- Beware of burnout.

- Remember that it is NOT perfect trying to be perfect!

- Be cautious of constant people pleasing. Break the addiction!

Exhaust Your Resources!

After completing the self-assessment from the book, list four of your biggest problem areas. List at least one strategy for "turning it around!"

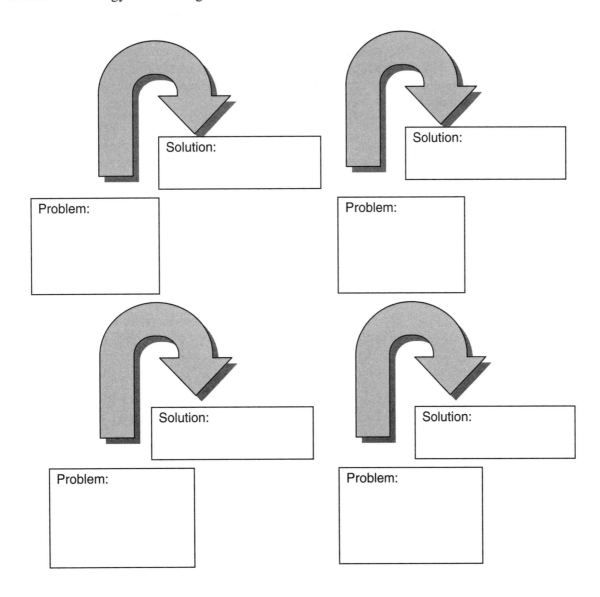

Solution:

Solution:

Problem:

Problem:

Solution:

Solution:

Problem:

Problem:

Lifesaver Tool #13

Pam's To-Do

LIFESAVER #14: Get Inside Organization!

Recommended Read: *Organizing from the Inside Out* by Julie Morgenstern.

Even if you've tried for years to get organized, it's not too late! Professional organizer Julie Morgenstern can help get your clutter under control. By taking stock of the situation, strategizing and creating a plan of action, and then attacking and getting the job done, you'll be on your way to conquering clutter in no time.

TIPS:

- Make a T-chart. On the left side of the paper, write a list of organizing strategies that are working. On the right side of the paper, write a list of organizing strategies that are clearly not working (see Lifesaver Tool #14.1).

- One of the reasons for procrastinating on getting organized is because of the time that it takes. Make a list of major organizing tasks that you need to tackle. Jot down an estimation of how much time you'll need to complete the task (i.e., sorting papers averages three hours . . . see Lifesaver Tool #14.2).

- Spend some time thinking about why you're not organized . . . then try to solve it. For example, if the biggest reason you're not organized is due to a lack of space, then it's a no-brainer to find space-saving solutions. If your biggest problem is a lack of time to organize, then blocking out time on Fridays to purge clutter would help. If you can determine the problem, it's easier to find a solution.

- See appendix A in Morgenstern's book for a complete list of organizing resources. You'll find toll-free numbers for At-a-Glance time savers and Staples Superstores and everything in between.

- Chapter 19 ("Taming Technology") is especially useful!

- Interested in an on-the-wall magnetic work board or schedule? These visual graphic organizers can help you see where your time is being spent! See chapter 18 ("Conquering the Clock").

What's Working? What's Not?

What's Working	What's Not Working

Lifesaver Tool #14.1

Chore Chart!

Chore	How Long Will It Take?
1.	
2.	
3.	
4.	
5.	

Lifesaver Tool #14.2

Our To-Do

LIFESAVER #15: No More Monkey Business!

Recommended Read: *The One-Minute Manager Meets the Monkey* by Kenneth H. Blanchard, William Oncken, and Hal Burrows.

"Do you have a minute?" As frustrating as that question can be during a busy day, it doesn't take much more than a minute to take control of your time. We wanted to book talk this book because it represents a problem that we both have had many times throughout our careers. We both are task-committed overachievers who others often seek out for help. Although we both believe in supporting others, we found that we often were the ones doing all the work. This book will help to get other peoples' problems (monkeys) off your back, while assisting them with problem-solving strategies and support. It really will keep your days from feeling like a zoo!

TIPS:

- Find ways to work smarter—not harder. Use Lifesaver Tool #15 (weekly task planner) as your personal time saver.

- Beware of solving other people's problems for them. Offering too much support can be enabling.

- Offer support, but provide problem-solving strategies.

- Provide training in reoccurring problem areas.

- Develop trust with your staff. High expectations will increase their productivity—and save yours.

- Delegate whenever possible—but have a follow-up system in place.

- Provide coaching support for important tasks and projects.

- Take control of your time—be proactive!

NO MORE MONKEY BUSINESS!
Weekly Task Planner

Problem: _____

    Delegation Plan: Target Date/Completed

    A: _____

    B: _____

    C: _____

    Comments/Next Steps:

Problem: _____

    Delegation Plan: Target Date/Completed

    A: _____

    B: _____

    C: _____

    Comments/Next Steps:

Lifesaver Tool #15

From *Library Lifesavers: A Survival Guide for Stressed Out Librarians* by Pamela S. Bacon and Tamora K. Bacon. Santa Barbara, CA: Libraries Unlimited. Copyright © 2010.

Tam's To-Do

LIFESAVER #16: Ready, Aim, Fire!

Recommended Read: *Teach Like Your Hair's on Fire* by Rafe Esquith.

The author of this book is humble and modest. He states, "Like all real teachers, I fail constantly. I don't get enough sleep. I lie awake in the early morning hours agonizing over a kid I was unable to reach. Being a teacher can be painful." Does this sound familiar? It did to me! I have always believed that discipline is really about building relationships. This book is a must-read from cover to cover!

The prologue left me teary-eyed as the author shared how his transformation occurred in his own career. As librarians, you will find the relationship-building and climate examples invaluable. The other sections offer invaluable ideas for teaching librarians and for collaboration with classroom teachers. I hope to use it as a study group book with my staff! (P.S.: I would like to think if the author met me, he would find that I don't fit the image of the literacy coach he describes in his book! Ouch!)

TIPS:

- First and foremost, build a climate of safety and trust.

- Discipline with fairness and high expectations.

- Be a positive role model and follow your "code of ethics"—especially when it is the most difficult.

- Help students develop joy, passion, and enthusiasm for reading!

- Keep writing! Practice does make perfect.

- Include project-based learning across all disciplines.

- Help students think for themselves and problem-solve.

- Promote positive relationships with students.

- Keep students highly engaged and connected with a heart for each other and for service.

- Keep your "flame" alive by using Lifesaver Tool #16.

Ready, Aim, Fire!

What "bright ideas" did you learn from this book that you could implement in your library or school?

Lifesaver Tool #16

Pam's To-Do

LIFESAVER #17: "Dewey" Discipline?

Recommended Read: *Discipline Survival Kit* by Julia G. Thompson.

When Pam found a survival guide for discipline packed with tools, techniques, and tips, she was "hooked." The book includes more than fifty reproducibles to be used immediately or easily adapted to deal with every discipline issue, large or small.

TIPS:

- This book focuses on helping the teacher-librarian move from the role of disciplinarian to facilitator or leader. Giving more control to the students may seem strange at first, but more student ownership and self-discipline is in the treasure chest when you find it!

- Student contracts can be an effective way to improve student behavior. When Pam had an especially troublesome study hall student, she drew up a behavior contract with him. Believe it or not, the student's behavior improved and, the next year, he even became a student helper! (Lifesaver Tool #17 is an example of a student contract.)

- Like Harry Wong suggests, being proactive with seating charts (or seating sections for the media center) and a warm welcome at the door can help you avoid many discipline problems.

- Use bell-to-bell instruction to prevent discipline problems. As we all know, when students have downtime, discipline problems can occur. Keep 'em busy—make every minute count!

- Building relationships is the best way to prevent discipline problems!

- Model positive behavior whenever possible.

- Know when to ignore (and when to ignore) discipline issues!

- Get your most difficult, uninspired students to take responsibility by planning engaging lessons.

- Give students a voice in the library classroom whenever possible. By giving students control, you'll give them more ownership and responsibility.

- Be sure to check out "50 Quick Ways to Reduce School Stress" on pages 348–350!

BEHAVIOR CONTRACT
"Be on Your Best Behavior!"

THIS CONTRACT IS MADE BETWEEN _____

(TEACHER/LIBRARIAN) AND _____(STUDENT).

THREE TARGET BEHAVIORS (BEHAVIORS TO IMPROVE):

1.

2.

3.

REWARDS IF BEHAVIOR IMPROVES:

_____

_____

_____

_____

_____

_____

_____

CONSEQUENCES IF BEHAVIOR DOES NOT IMPROVE:

_____

_____

_____

_____

_____

_____

CHECK-UPS WILL BE DONE: WEEKLY MONTHLY OTHER (CIRCLE ONE)

THE NEXT CHECK-UP WILL BE ON:
_____.

TEACHER SIGNATURE: STUDENT SIGNATURE:

_____   _____

Lifesaver Tool #17

Tam's To-Do

LIFESAVER #18: Have You Tried "Dignified?"

Recommended Read: *Discipline with Dignity* by Richard L. Curwin and Allen N. Mendler.

I believe I speak for us all when I say that I wish there was a "magic recipe" for handling all student discipline problems—perhaps even a special "magic dust" that could be sprinkled over the students as they enter your school or library. This book speaks to the importance of school staff creating their own social contracts with students that are highly individualized to meet the individual needs of today's kids. The strategies encourage you to think outside of the box in order to create a culture and climate for learning!

TIPS:

- Allow student input when developing your social contract.

- Remember that choice is very powerful.

- Teach students (and yourself) to reframe negative situations.

- Diffuse power struggles. Don't be afraid to use humor to desist difficult situations.

- Build relationships with students! (Sound familiar?)

- Don't expect a one-size-fits-all approach to work—be fair, which doesn't mean "equal."

- Model what you expect—give respect in order to get it!

- Remember that responsibility is more important than obedience—teach it!

- Do everything possible to keep a child's dignity intact.

- Use proximity as a proactive measure.

- Seek creative solutions to problem behaviors—include the students in brainstorming possible solutions. Use Lifesaver Tool #18 to document student comments.

Have You Tried "Dignified?"

Ask a trustworthy student helper to write down a few comments from students to help you see how your library's climate is viewed by your "customers!"

What do you think about the climate of the library?

Lifesaver Tool #18

Pam's To-Do

LIFESAVER #19: Get Out Your Toolkit!

Recommended Read: *Fred Jones Tools for Teaching: Discipline, Instruction, and Motivation* by Frederic H. Jones.

When this book promised skills for me, and other exceptional/experienced teacher-librarians, to transform my library media center into a place of success and enjoyment for both myself and my students, I was intrigued and a little skeptical. I must say, however, that the book did reveal techniques that reduced my stress level by providing solid classroom-management strategies. I found that by reducing the amount of little annoyances (back talkers, interrupters, and hand raisers), I was more prepared to deal with the bigger discipline issues.

TIPS:

- Purchase the second edition, which includes an overview DVD, parent videos, and an activity guide. These resources are perfect for small group workshops for either teachers or with parents for a community resource.

- Recommend this book for rookies or veterans. I read it as a veteran teacher-librarian and picked up several useful strategies.

- If your library ever floods (mine did!) and you have to take one discipline-related book with you, this is the one to grab! The book is helpful with discipline strategies, but it also helps teachers improve classroom instruction which, in turn, reduces discipline problems.

- Learn how to make students (not you!) work harder . . . you're already working hard enough!

- Find out how using simple proximity (closeness) can prevent discipline issues without having to say a word! Use Lifesaver Tool #19 to document your discipline progress.

- Start a *Tools for Teaching* study group. Go to http://www.fredjones.com for more information.

Teacher Toolbox

In *Tools for Teaching*, the "Praise, Prompt, and Leave" (or, as I like to refer to it, simply PPL) strategy is key. PPL is a technique that the teacher uses to give positive feedback (praise), a suggestion for improvement (prompt), and make a quick exit (leave), especially for clingy or needy students. This strategy encourages the "helpless hand raisers" to gain independence and allows the teacher to focus on all students, not just a few of the more vocal ones.

Directions: Record your efforts using the PPL strategy. Practice with the same student to monitor progress . . . or practice with different students to gain experience and effectiveness in using this new strategy.

Practice #1: Praise, Prompt, and Leave

Practice #2: Praise, Prompt, and Leave

Practice #3: Praise, Prompt, and Leave

Lifesaver Tool #19

Our To-Do

LIFESAVER #20: Hold On a Minute!

Recommended Read: *One-Minute Discipline* by Arnie Bianco

We are all looking for quick strategies that really work! This book is full of ideas that you can pick up and use immediately. In addition, it is a great tool for your professional library to support your staff. It takes just a minute!

TIPS:

- Consider adapting the survey on pages 30–31 to get student feedback on the atmosphere in your library. Use Lifesaver Tool #20 as an activity to promote student climate.

- Review the characteristics of a healthy classroom. Do these seem to reflect your library? What goals would you like to add?

- Consider the teacher reminders on page 50—are these reflected in your library, your school, and your district?

- Take part in parent conferences of your best and hardest students!

- Document issues and provide copies to the child and to the classroom teacher and principal.

- Take the "Teacher Oath" on page 82—keep it handy as a reference tool!

- Teach and practice your routines and procedures—in the beginning of the year, during the semester, and as a review when needed.

- Be creative with incentives—brainstorm ideas with students and have a "menu" of options for rewarding and reinforcing positive behavior.

- Be a "survivor!" Section 9 includes a wealth of ideas on how you can deal with stressors—a must for busy librarians!

- Form a support group! Both you and your staff will appreciate all of the reproducible forms in Section 10. They will save you invaluable time and energy and only take a "minute!"

Hold on a Minute!

Use this form as a "getting-to-know-you" partner activity in the beginning of the year with students. Collect them and keep them as handy references for relationship building with difficult students later in the year.

1. **What is your favorite song or artist?**

2. **What is your favorite sport or hobby?**

3. **What is your favorite season?**

4. **Do you collect anything?**

5. **What is your funniest memory?**

6. **Are you a morning person or a night owl?**

7. **What is your favorite subject? Least favorite?**

8. **What would I be surprised to know about you?**

TALK ABOUT IT: COUNSELOR'S CORNER

Prior to having twins, raising toddlers, and taking care of two teens, one of my favorite ways to relax and renew was with a great book! Like many of you, I like to catch Oprah's top picks and I can honestly say that the book *A New Earth-Awakening to Your Life's Purpose* by Eckhart Tolle really changed my life. I encourage you to read and reflect on this book and be open to its power.

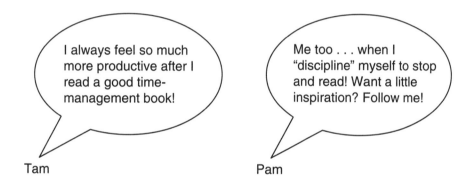

I always feel so much more productive after I read a good time-management book!

Tam

Me too . . . when I "discipline" myself to stop and read! Want a little inspiration? Follow me!

Pam

Think and Reflect: Journal Prompt

True renewal starts from within. We know that reading opens doors and inspires new ideas.

Reflect on the readings from this chapter. List the "aha" ideas and page numbers that you may want to remember for future reference.

_____
_____
_____
_____
_____
_____
_____
_____
_____
_____
_____
_____
_____
_____
_____
_____
_____
_____
_____
_____
_____
_____
_____
_____
_____
_____
_____
_____
_____
_____
_____
_____

Chapter 4

Inspire and Invigorate . . . Yourself and Others

Lifesaver Chapter 4

Inspire and Invigorate . . . Yourself and Others

Talk

Q. It seems like the teachers and staff who come into the library are usually negative and our school seems to have more and more problems with low morale. How can I help to inspire them—as well as myself?

—Tired, Not Inspired Librarian

I have always found that the best way to inspire others (and motivate myself) is through **talking** and **networking** with others and connecting on a personal level.

Tam

You do like to talk. On the other hand, I've always found the key to inspiring and supporting others is by **listening**!

Pam

Take the Tests!

I	**I** can easily think of three people who inspire me. Name them! 1. 2. 3.
N	**N**egative situations do not ruin my day. Provide example:
S	**S**tudy groups are an ongoing part of my library media center program. Topic of current study group:_____
P	**P**eople often comment on how positive I am. List two people below who have commented recently. 1. 2.
I	**I**f I could change or inspire just one negative person in my school, I would choose_____.
R	**R**eading inspirational articles is a regular part of my weekly schedule. Last inspirational article read:_____
E	**E**ven when times are tough, I stay positive. Provide example here:

Now that you're INSPIRED, let's see if we can INVIGORATE you!

Directions: Answer Yes (Y) or No (N) on each of the statements below.

I	If someone were to comment on your energy level, they would say it was usually high. YES OR NO
N	Napping is a way to invigorate myself. YES OR NO
V	Vitamins are routine for me. YES OR NO
I	I look at myself as a person with excess energy. YES OR NO
G	Getting regular exercise is important to me. YES OR NO
O	On most days, I wake up well rested and refreshed. YES OR NO
R	Relaxing is as important to me as exercising. YES OR NO
A	A balance in all areas of my life (personal and professional) is key. YES OR NO
T	Taking minibreaks to invigorate myself is part of my daily routine. YES OR NO
E	Energy bars and/or healthy snacks are always in my desk. YES OR NO

Author's Note: Tam and I each completed the second "Take the Test!" See our INVIGORATE answers on Lifesaver Tools #20.1 and #20.2. PB

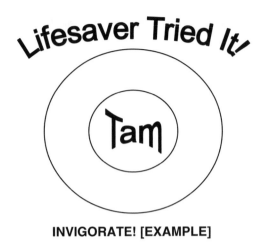

INVIGORATE! [EXAMPLE]

Test Yourself

Directions: Answer yes (Y) or no (N) for each of the statements below.

If someone were to comment on your energy level, they would say it was usually high.
Yes—others often comment on my enthusiasm and "bubbly personality."

Napping is a way to invigorate myself.
Yes—although I take more of a "power nap" than Pam, who hibernates!

Vitamins are routine for me.
I have gotten out of my routine of taking my extra calcium—set a goal.

I look at myself as a person with excess energy.
No! Set a goal to get back into the fitness center and be more consistent. May is a month where I need to work out the most, but haven't!

Getting regular exercise is important to me.
Yes—I feel and look better!

On most days, I wake up well rested and refreshed.
Yes! We splurged on a new Sleep Number bed and high thread-count sheets and it was money well spent!

Relaxing is as important to me as exercising.
Set a goal—I do believe that I need to be more proactive in this area—especially while raising teens!

Lifesaver Tool #20.1

A balance in all areas of my life (personal and professional) is key.
Definitely! I notice when I am out of balance in my work life, the other areas of my life become out of synch. (Refer to chapter 3 for great strategies on time management.)

Taking mini breaks to invigorate myself is part of my daily routine.
I have just started scheduling a "mini break" on my calendar for the mid-morning, when I have a bottle of water and a power bar. I listen to some relaxing music and try to turn off my mind for a few moments . . . it really helps during a hectic day.

Energy bars and/or healthy snacks are always in my desk.
Yes! My office is right next to the teacher's lounge, where chocolate is sold! I find I am less tempted when I plan ahead for a healthy alternative.

Exercising our mouths and bodies is a way that Tam (right) and I INVIGORATE ourselves!
Author's Note: I finished the trail first! ☺ PB

Lifesaver Tool #20.1

From Library Lifesavers: A Survival Guide for Stressed Out Librarians by Pamela S. Bacon and Tamora K. Bacon. Santa Barbara, CA: Libraries Unlimited. Copyright © 2010.

INVIGORATE! (EXAMPLE)

Test Yourself

Directions: Answer yes (Y) or no (N) for each of the statements below.

IF someone were to comment on your energy level, they would say it was usually high.
Yes! In public, I tend to be somewhat hyper. I'm bubbly and energetic. At home, I'm more of a slug (but no one sees that!).

Napping is a way to invigorate myself.
Yes! I take long naps (two hours is my average!).

Vitamins are routine for me.
Yes! After talking with my friends, I am often surprised how many people don't take vitamins regularly. Taking a multivitamin, calcium, and vitamin B are a regular part of my nightly routine.

I look at myself as a person with excess energy.
Not really. At home, I tend to be somewhat sluggish. It's like my energy is used up throughout the week and I don't have any left by the weekend. A goal is to exercise more and eat healthier in an attempt to have more energy and become more fit.

Getting regular exercise is important to me.
While I agree that it is very important, I struggle to exercise regularly. It's a goal!

On most days, I wake up well rested and refreshed.
Not really. I am NOT a morning person. Even though I get plenty of sleep (eight hours), I don't wake up refreshed. I wake up grouchy! (Don't let Tam fool you by her answer . . . she is horrible until she has her two cups of coffee!).

Relaxing is as important to me as exercising.
Yes! Although I sometimes slack in the exercise category, I regularly read and nap!

Lifesaver Tool #20.2

A balance in all areas of my life (personal and professional) is key.
Yes! This is a goal area. I am continually striving to create balance.

Taking mini breaks to invigorate myself is part of my daily routine.
Not yet. This is a goal area.

Energy bars and/or healthy snacks are always in my desk.
Yes! I bring bottled water and a low-carb, healthy snack with me every day to work. I try to stay away from the vending machines at school whenever possible (too tempting!).

Author's Note: Pam only finished the trail first because I was taking this inspirational picture! TB

Lifesaver Tool #20.2

Tam's To-Do

LIFESAVER #21: Get It "Booked!"

There are definitely two types of study groups or book clubs—the "have tos" and the "want tos." Although they both have an important purpose, the book club that you attend because you "want to" is definitely much more fun and inspiring! After having participated in (and even taken a lead role) in a required school study group over a professional reading, I was a little hesitant after I was asked to join a social book club. I wondered if it would be something I would actually enjoy since I already, quite literally, had my hands full of professional books and journals waiting to be "read and led." I know that many educators and librarians feel this way! However, after joining and attending my first meeting, I can emphatically say that the networking and relaxed social atmosphere was just what I needed. I left the meeting inspired to begin planning my own group read!

TIPS:

- If you are starting a group from scratch, think carefully about whom to include. You want to be sure that the personalities of the group mix well. (Similar to when making student groups!)

- Reflect! Think about what made other book clubs fun and inspiring—and what did not.

- What unique location(s) do you have to offer? For example: I am known for my lake-themed book clubs, where we have our meetings on a boat!

- Decide on your book of choice and begin planning your theme. (Use Lifesaver #21 as a book club planning form. Check out Lifesaver #21.2 for a Tried It example!)

- Be sure to bring your calendar to the meeting so that others can sign up for a date/time to host their book club meeting after you have inspired them to give it a try!

"Get It 'Booked!'"
Book Club Planner

Guests:

Study Group Book Title(s):

Theme:

Possible Date(s):

Food and Drinks:

Supplies Needed:

"Get it Booked!"
Book Club Planner (Example)

Media Specialist Amy Weliever

Guests:

(Names withheld to protect the innocent—just kidding!)

Study Group Book Title(s): *Twilight* **by Stephanie Meyer**

Theme: **Darkness**
(Guests were asked to wear black and, as favors, the hostess gifted black nail polish. Several members chose to buy posters from the movie to display around the book club site).

Possible Date(s):

Last day of school!

Food and Drinks:

Book club night featured theme-related delicacies: pasta with red sauce, red drink choices, chocolate fountains with white chocolate and red food coloring, just to name a few of the appetizers guests wanted to quickly take a "bite" out of.

Supplies Needed:
Paper products
Book study questions

Lifesaver Tool #21.2

Pam's To-Do

LIFESAVER #22: No Meetings Allowed!

Want a club where you meet face-to-face and discuss professional books with other members? If so, the online-only book club (OOBC) is **not** for you! Although Tam's book club (see above) does meet, socialize, and discuss inspiring books, this club is online only. After all, who needs even one more meeting to go to?

TIPS:

- Send out an e-mail to colleagues announcing the OOBC.

- Choose an inspirational professional book to promote.

- Post a reading schedule online.

- Hold weekly (optional!) "meetings" online for those chatty types (like Tam!) who want to have book-related discussions.

- After reading, provide a rating form (see Lifesaver Tool #22) for readers to let others know whether they will be inspired . . . or not . . . after reading the book.

- Encourage other potential group members to "join" next time. It's a great way to get through those "have-to" reads with a little inspiration!

Online-Only Book Club Rating Form

Please complete and turn in this month's rating form to _____ by_____.

Book Title:

Author:

1. I found this book to be inspiring.

Yes   Somewhat   No

2. I would recommend this book to a friend or coworker.

Yes   Somewhat   No

3. This book was easy to read and hard to put down.

Yes   Somewhat   No

*On the back, write a brief note about your overall opinion of the book. What makes it a "must" read or a "must-not" read?

I would like to have an online chat about this book:

Yes No

Best times/possible dates:

Lifesaver #22

Tam's To-Do

LIFESAVER #23: "Well"—Why not?

As librarians and educators, we are more and more burdened with a million tasks and responsibilities. At times, wellness seems to be at the bottom of the priority list. However, if it stays there for long, our bodies and minds will suffer. I find inspiration in teams and groups for synergy! At my school, we have made a "wellness team" that encourages and motivates us to make healthy choices and stay focused on our goals. By inspiring each other (even if it means giving the nonverbal glare as I reach for a donut), the team support goes beyond what I could do independently.

TIPS:

- Mailbox messages for inspiration help provide team support and encouragement.

- Several online sites offer inspirational ideas to pass on to a friend or coworker who needs a lift.

- Consider using Lifesaver #23 for a wellness group reporting form.

- Add a challenge! We have found that friendly competition for weight loss or a running competition, etc., keeps the motivation going.

- Be open to the group ideas for ways to celebrate often!

"Well? Why Not?"
Wellness Group Survey

Name:_____

I am interested in learning more about:

Health and fitness
Inspiration/motivational strategies
Handling stress
Time-saving strategies
Creating balance

Other:

Are you an "expert" in a certain area that could help inspire others? Would you consider leading a group meeting?

What self-help book(s) do you consider a must-read for others?

What do you consider to be your biggest hurdle or obstacle right now, personally or professionally?

Would you like to be linked with an "inspiration partner" to help celebrate and motivate each other? Yes   No

Lifesaver Tool #23

Pam's To-Do

LIFESAVER #24: Socializing: Eat It Up!

Socializing is a great way to get inspired—and a perfect opportunity to inspire others. At our school, teacher Shannon Rose serves as our social chairman. She performs many social tasks and acts as our department cheerleader. One of her favorite functions, however, is organizing our monthly food days. You might not think that a simple pitch-in is a way to relieve stress or inspire others, but I beg to differ. Being a part of a school family helps you feel less stressed and isolated. You're no longer disconnected—you're a valuable member of the food chain (pun intended)! Getting together with colleagues you respect is fun and stress-relieving (there's comfort knowing others are just as stressed as you!). Sometimes just being able to listen while you break bread is inspiring all by itself.

TIPS:

- To get more food-day participation, choose a theme (see Lifesaver Tool #24 for a form to organize food-day themes).

- Send out constant reminders (we forget—sorry, Shannon).

- Send out mailbox messages reminding teachers of the upcoming event.

- Don't give up if the first few food days aren't successful.

- At food days (or any social event), take photos to post on your department bulletin board. It's fun to laugh at all the silly pictures.

- Host a food day yearly in the library and show off those new books!

- Tried and True Favorites:

  - Brunch for Lunch
  - Mexican Fiesta
  - Tailgate Party
  - Chili Cookoff

Food Fun Days

Directions: The dates and themes for this semester's food fun days are listed below. Please sign up on one of the "benches" if you can help organize the special event!

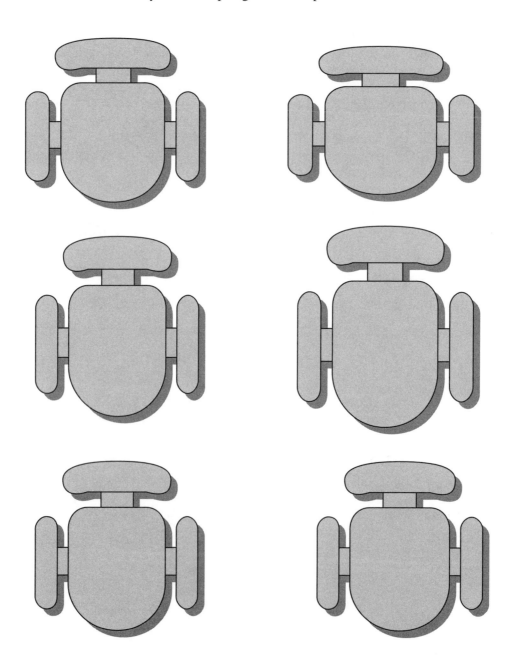

Lifesaver #24

Our To-Do

LIFESAVER #25: We're "Positive" About This!

People often comment on how positive we both are both in and out of the school setting! We often discuss how it is funny that sometimes we don't really "feel" as positive as we are perceived. Although it isn't always easy to be positive—it is vitally important to staff members, and especially students, to try our best. How do we do it? Check out the tips below and see if they inspire you to "put on a happy face!"

TIPS:

- Be a "need meeter" and try to help others when they need it most!

- Have a spirit of giving— both personally and professionally.

- Be supportive and encouraging.

- Don't confuse being positive with being a "doormat." The key is to change your attitude about the things that you can control.

- Be dependable and follow through—you will be an inspiration to others when they know they can count on you.

- Be a problem-solver! Rather than procrastinate and worry, be creative and think about how to solve the problem in a win-win way.

- Try to be an inspiration to others, yet be inspired by others! (Lifesaver Tool #25 gives you a place to record professional and personal acts of inspiration.)

"You're My Inspiration!"

Directions: Reflect on the impact that you have on others, both personally and professionally. List and date the people and/or situations that come to mind. Keep this as a celebration and reflection of your goals in this area.

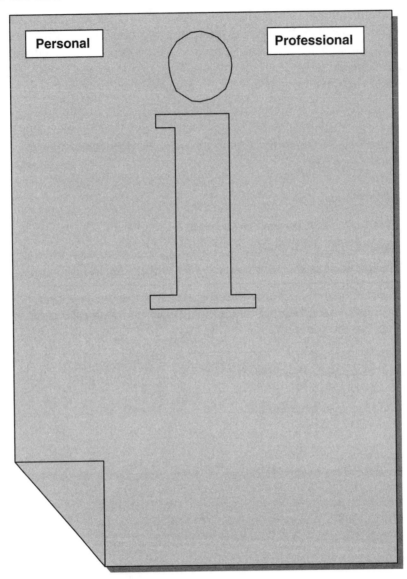

Lifesaver Tool #25

TALK ABOUT IT: COUNSELOR'S CORNER

Although I feel one of my most important goals in both my work and my family life is to inspire others, it is equally important that we recognize our own needs for inspiration. Nothing steals our joy and peace like a cluttered schedule. I encourage you to find what inspires you, both personally and professionally, and make that time for yourself! I know that those around me benefit most when I remember to "practice what I preach!"

Think and Reflect: Journal Prompt

You have what it takes to inspire and invigorate yourself . . . and others!

Refer to your test. What new goals would you like to set for yourself in this area? Meet with a friend or colleague and hold yourself accountable to taking the action steps that you set for yourself.

Chapter 5

View . . . Looking Out After Looking In

Lifesaver Chapter 5

 **View . . . Looking Out After Looking In**

Talk

Q. Help! I'm in a rut! I know I need to refocus and be more reflective, but I'm just too tired (yawn).
—Listless Librarian

> I recommend that you take a little time out for yourself to reflect on where you are . . . and where you're going. By focusing on your **future**, you'll start to recognize if (and when) you need to change directions.

Tam

> I can "see" the need to look at the future, but what about the **present**? I think she needs to take immediate action—and "view" herself with new eyes.

Pam

Take the Test!

HOW DO YOU SEE YOURSELF? FIND OUT NOW!		
1. My outer view and my inner view closely relate.		
Rarely ☹	Sometimes	Usually ☺
2. I see myself happy in my current position in five years.		
Rarely ☹	Sometimes	Usually ☺
3. I'm happy with the way I view myself.		
Rarely ☹	Sometimes	Usually ☺
4. I'm happy with the way I view the world.		
Rarely ☹	Sometimes	Usually ☺
5. Others view me as a positive person.		
Rarely ☹	Sometimes	Usually ☺

Scoring guide: The goal is to have all "usually" answers. This reflective test can be used often as a vision checkup.

Tam's To-Do

LIFESAVER #26: Vision Notebook: View Your Future!

I first saw a vision notebook used by a friend when she was planning her wedding. I was amazed by how a simple three-ring binder, plastic sleeves, and magazine cutouts could be used to create the perfect vision for what she wanted. When I attended the wedding, it was just like flipping through the pages of her notebook! I realized that by specifically visualizing what she wanted, she had been able to transform her life.

Throughout the years, I have used my own vision notebook to help me visualize where I am—and where I want to be, both personally and professionally. Typically, I take a mini-retreat once each year with my sister to reflect, review, and revise my vision notebook. I encourage you to create your own (see Lifesaver Tool #26 for a vision notebook action planning sheet and reflection tool).

TIPS:

- Decide on your personal style. Do you prefer a binder, journal, poster board, etc?

- Reflect! Take some quiet time for yourself to begin to reflect on what you really want. Brainstorm a list of what makes you happy. Where do you find joy? What would bring you more joy? Reflecting on these types of questions helps you to start getting a visual image of the life you want for yourself.

- After visualizing your ideas, find pictures that represent what you want to achieve.

- Make an action plan with specific target goals (see Lifesaver Tool #26). Ask yourself: Does your current position, lifestyle, and personal life match your vision?

- Place your vision notebook/poster in a prominent place and revisit it often as you begin taking action on your goals.

"View Your Future!"
Action Plan

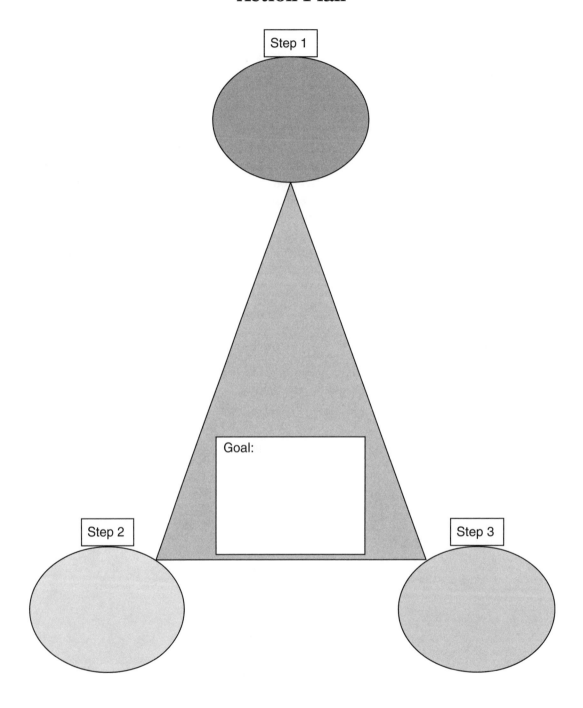

Lifesaver Tool #26

Pam's To-Do

LIFESAVER #27: Candid Camera: View Your Present

How do you see yourself? Are your lenses foggy? This activity helps you see yourself as you really are. I am as camera-phobic as the next person (Tam, of course, is a total ham in front of the camera), but this activity truly helped me see myself in a different way. For example, a picture taken at a department meeting shows me looking bored and disengaged. Upon reflection, I realized that I was growing out of my current role and felt somewhat trapped. A picture taken of me with students, however, was totally different. I looked happy, energized, and invigorated; I saw myself where I really wanted to be—making a difference daily in the lives of students. This viewpoint helped me see that, for now anyway, I wanted to get back into more of a teaching role and get out of some of my ever-increasing committee responsibilities.

TIPS:

- Buy two disposable digital cameras.

- Give one camera to your best friend.

- Give one camera to your best colleague.

- Ask your photographers to take candid pictures of you. These should be "real" action photos of you—not posed! The goal is to get a variety of pictures of you in both your personal and professional life.

- Develop the photos. If possible, have photos put onto a CD for computer viewing.

- View the photos critically. Take notes on how you see yourself (Lifesaver Tool #27.1 provides forms to post your pictures and comments).

- Lifesaver Tool #27.2 features my mentor and inspiration, Nancy Witty. Nancy's Tried It shows that this lifesaver is really a "snap!"

- What do you like? What would you like to see changed? Do the pictures reflect who you'd really like to be?

- Ask a friend to take a critical look at the photos. When they look at you, what do they see? What do they think should stay the same? What do they think you should change?

- Reflect on what you have seen.

Candid Camera: View Your Present

Directions: Paste a photo in the space below. Label the picture and provide a brief reflection of your reaction to looking at yourself in full view. Do you like what you see?

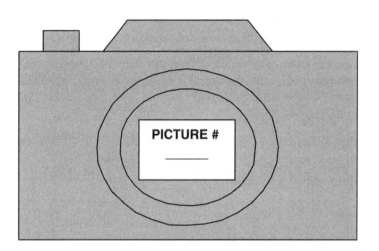

PHOTO REFLECTION . . .

Lifesaver Tool #27.1

Candid Camera: View Your Present
(Example)

Directions: Paste a photo in the space below. Label the picture and provide a brief reflection of your reaction to looking at yourself in full view. Do you like what you see?

Tool twist: Have a favorite coworker comment for an objective view (example below).

Media Specialist Nancy Witty

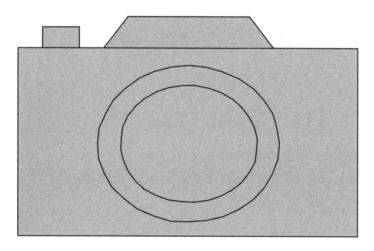

PHOTO REFLECTION . . .
This picture is a typical workday photo of Nancy. Her bright smile, bubbly personality, and willingness to stop everything she's doing (even just for a photo shoot!) is just part of what makes her such a success at Rockville Elementary. Even caught off-guard, Nancy's office is organized, functional, and welcoming. No wonder she's my mentor and inspiration! —PB

Lifesaver Tool #27.2

Tam's To-Do

Lifesaver #28: View Yourself and Your Surroundings With Passion

When you are buried under a mound of work at your desk, it is difficult to imagine picturing anything else! This section is all about changing your outlook by changing your view. I was able to experience a similar activity like this at an administrator's retreat a few years ago. I remember that I was feeling very burdened by some personal problems, as well as stressed from working too many hours in the office. After a counselor led us through a positive visualization activity, I couldn't believe how much more renewed I felt. I encourage you to "see" it for yourself.

TIPS:

- Reflect on a location that you feel passionate about . . . this could include a picture from a special vacation or a location that you aspire to visit.

- Visualize yourself there.

- Be specific with your feelings—how does it make your feel?

- Picture it in your mind so that you can "go there" anytime you are feeling especially stressed or burnt out.

- Keep this picture in a frame on your desk to remind you to take a moment for yourself to reflect and relax!

- Use Lifesaver Tool #28 to document your passionate place.

Your Passionate Place

When you look at your picture and "play the movie in your mind," think about how that passionate place makes you feel. Take a moment to list those key words on the chart below. You may be inspired to list a special quote as well. Use this tool as a reminder to give yourself a mind break in your hectic day!

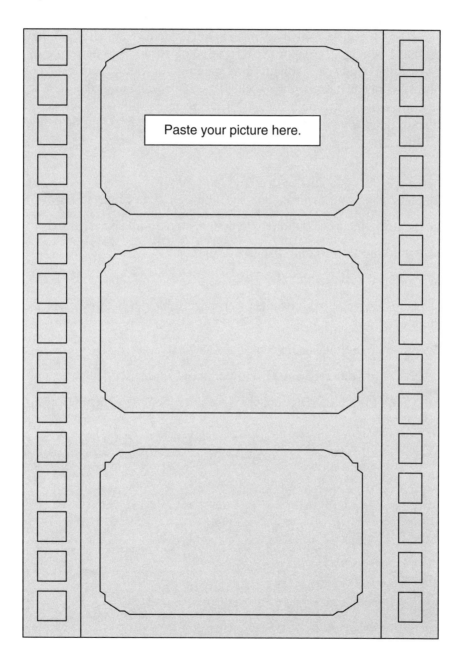

Paste your picture here.

Lifesaver Tool #28

Pam's To-Do

Lifesaver #29: View Yourself as a Professional

Sometimes stress levels improve with a little personal and/or professional recognition—even if you have to be the source of that recognition. For example, every time I publish a book or an article, I send a little e-mail to my superintendent. Sure, it's patting myself on the back a little, but I believe it's important for the administration to be aware of the hard work I'm doing—and the valuable publicity I'm gaining for our school and community. This improves the view of our program's stakeholders while validating the view I have of myself as I celebrate my writing accomplishments. The special purple pen I always get from the superintendent gives me something to jot down new writing ideas and helps me view my program with "giant" pride.

TIPS:

- Take pictures of your students and staff during media center visits.

- Take pictures with your digital (or video) camera at all special events.

- Create scrolling PowerPoint displays of photos.

- Post photos on bulletin boards.

- Post photos on your media center web page (change pictures often to encourage site visitors!).

- Include photos in your media center newsletter.

- Send photos to your central office to be placed in district newsletters or flyers.

- Send photos to the local newspaper. Lifesaver Tool #29 includes a ready-to-use press release format.

Your Professional View

(Press Release Template)

	For More Information, Contact:
Month, Date, Year	Name
	Title
School	Telephone Number
	E-mail Address

FOR IMMEDIATE RELEASE

TITLE: _____

Paragraph One (City, State)

State who, what, where, when.

Paragraph Two

Include more information about the event or activity.

If you are the spokesperson for the event or activity, include a relevant quotation here.

Paragraph Three

Place other information here (whom to contact for more information, how to get involved, etc.)

Final Paragraph

Include your school/organization's logo and motto here.

Lifesaver Tool #29

Our To-Do

Lifesaver #30: View Your Present and Future Possibilities

While you may have noticed that we often don't agree on the same strategies and "view" things differently, this lifesaver is one that we can both approve wholeheartedly (very rare)! We each had the unique opportunity to create new positions for ourselves within our current school corporations. While I was principal, I wrote a proposal to receive certification as a literacy coordinator in order to fulfill my dream of working exclusively in the area of professional development. On the other hand, Pam was able to transition into a position that allows her to focus solely on struggling readers, which she "sees" as her passion.

TIPS:

- Review your test answers (see above). What did you learn?

- List possible career goals . . . one year, five years, or ten years. Do your goals change or remain consistent with where you are now?

- Consider what additional training, workshops, certifications, or courses you may need in order to fulfill your goals.

- Don't be afraid to take a risk and try something new.

- Interview someone you admire who is in a different role. Talk to them and reflect on what this might look like for you.

- If you plan on staying in your present position long term, consider smaller, but important, changes you can make that will enhance the view of your surroundings.

- Take time to visualize yourself in different, perhaps unfamiliar, surroundings. By visualizing, you can begin to see yourself in a new way.

- Lifesaver Tool #30 helps you view yourself now and in the future.

Present and Future Views

Directions: Take a "snapshot" in your mind's eye . . . view yourself where you are and where you want to go. Jot down some thoughts on the chart below. Be sure to include the date beside your notes. Your "view" may change if you do this same activity a year from now! Keeping the date helps you "see" changes when they occur.

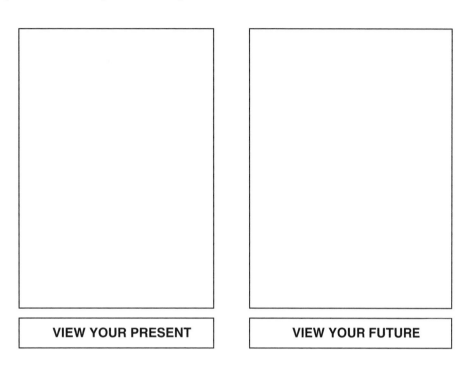

ARE YOUR VIEWS THE SAME . . . OR DIFFERENT?
IT'S UP TO YOU . . . CHOOSE YOUR VIEW!

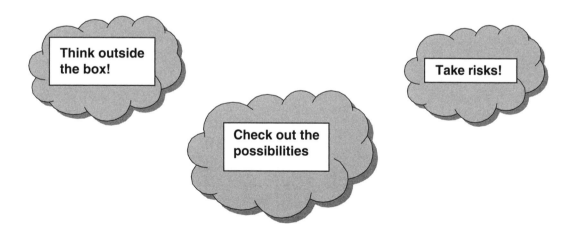

Lifesaver Tool #30

TALK ABOUT IT: COUNSELOR'S CORNER

As a counselor, I have read several books on the importance of having a positive attitude and visualization. As an adult, I found *The Secret* by Rhonda Byrne to be a book that reaffirmed my beliefs. I believe that you will find that the law of attraction is no "secret" to a successful life!

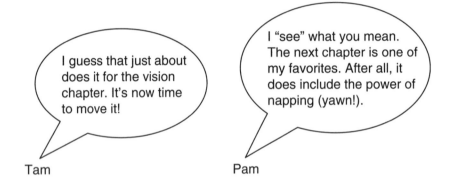

I guess that just about does it for the vision chapter. It's now time to move it!

Tam

I "see" what you mean. The next chapter is one of my favorites. After all, it does include the power of napping (yawn!).

Pam

Think and Reflect: Journal Prompt

Viewing yourself differently will emerge only from a place deep within.

Go to that deep place and reflect upon the view of yourself that you have after reading and reflecting on this chapter.

_____
_____
_____
_____
_____
_____
_____
_____
_____
_____
_____
_____
_____
_____
_____
_____
_____
_____
_____
_____
_____
_____
_____
_____
_____
_____
_____
_____

Chapter 6

Exercise . . . Your Mind and Body

Exercise . . . Your Mind and Body

Talk

Q. Help! I go between three buildings and feel constantly pulled in different directions. With work, home, and a million other responsibilities, I feel emotionally and physically exhausted all the time. The last thing I feel like doing is working out. What can I do?

—Tired Teacher-Librarian

> I would try getting your groove on by listening to some great music. Take this a "step" further by walking, jogging, or even dancing to your favorite tune. The important thing is to get your body moving!

Tam

> Getting your body moving is great, but stopping to rest your mind may need to be your first "step." After your mind is at rest, your body may be ready to get moving!

Pam

Take the Test!

WHEN IS THE BEST TIME TO EXERCISE . . . YOUR BODY?		
1. You like to exercise in the morning to wake up.	T	F
2. You like to exercise after a long day to relax and unwind.	T	F
3. You like to exercise in the morning to make sure you get it done.	T	F
4. You like to exercise your body to be more productive for a long night ahead.	T	F
5. You like to wind down after a hectic day and not get too keyed up.	T	F
6. You want to exercise to boost your metabolism.	T	F

WHEN IS THE BEST TIME TO EXERCISE . . . YOUR MIND?		
7. You like to start your day off with some personal and spiritual "think" time.	T	F
8. You like to end your day with some peaceful reflection and meditation.	T	F
9. You like to take mini mind breaks during the day to boost your productivity.	T	F
10. You like to meditate and relax your mind before going to sleep.	T	F

If you answered "true" for the following numbers, morning exercise and meditation are the best for you:
1, 3, 5, 6*, 7, 9*

If you answered "false" for the following numbers, evening exercise and meditation are the best for you:
2, 4, 6*, 8, 9*

*Note: Questions #6 and #9 are equally correct for both categories. Exercising during <u>any</u> time of the day is an effective way to boost metabolism . . . and using meditation at any time is a great way to boost your productivity!

Tam's To-Do

LIFESAVER #31: Listen to Music . . . Just Dance!

With each new school year, I set new goals and begin them in earnest! However, I used to find that by the end of the first month, I was both physically and mentally worn out. The last thing that I wanted to do was work out! For me, that changed when I became a "Zumba" fan! Zumba is a dance class filled with inspirational and upbeat Latin music that really helped me get my groove back. In addition, I found that by listening to my favorite songs while I was walking or jogging, I could go for longer periods of time and found that my attitude became more positive when I returned to work. Often, I found that I could even go back to work later that evening and my productivity was so much better. Soon, you might find yourself whistling a happy tune!

TIPS:

- Use Lifesaver Tool #31 to brainstorm music that inspires you to get moving!

- Reflect on what type of class(es) might help you to get your groove on.

- Surround yourself with other "groupies" who enjoy dancing and/or the same type of music—share CDs.

- Start slow when becoming active . . . perhaps walk with intermittent spurts of jogging until you work up to your own level of optimal (and optimistic!) performance.

- Sing in the car! (Warning: Teenagers find parents who sing very embarrassing and irritating—they, however, are very talented and can sing at any time at very high volume.)

- Purchase your own iPod or MP3 player and download your "old favorites!" After listening to some 1980s music, I am often ready to solve my toughest problems.

- Listen to motivational (for me, it is spiritual) music while getting ready in the morning. This is a great way to start the day on a positive "note!"

"You've Got to Move It, Move It!"

Brainstorm a list of "old favorites" that inspire you to dance!

Brainstorm a list of new songs or artists that you might try . . .

Reflect on how you feel before after you "dance to the beat!"

Lifesaver Tool #31

Pam's To-Do

LIFESAVER #32: Listen to Yourself . . . or Nothing at All!

Too many times our minds are racing with our thoughts, our to-dos, or our troubles. Sometimes even your favorite music can add noise to an already over-stimulated mind. Take a mental time-out to listen to . . . nothing. When you take time to embrace the silence, you'll be surprised by what you hear.

TIPS:

- If you find it hard to listen to nothing at first, then start quietly by playing some soft, background ambient music. I especially like the sound of the ocean waves crashing out of my boom box.

- As you begin your quiet-time routine, check out a copy of *Yoga for Dummies* from your public library. Learning some simple yoga moves can help you learn to stretch your mind and your body.

- Build some deep breathing into your relaxation routine. The Lifesaver Tool on yoga below provides step-by-step instructions to help you get the most out of your stretching . . . you'll never be out of breath!

- Don't worry if you find it hard to relax at first. Many people who are especially wound up and feeling stressed take longer to learn relaxation strategies (I'm still learning!).

- When you start deep breathing, you may feel a little light-headed because of all of the oxygen flowing into your body. Not to worry . . . just take it slow and easy.

- Use Lifesaver Tool #32 to record how you feel before you begin your quiet time and/ or meditation practice. What is your mood (angry, sad, tired, happy, excited . . .)? How are you feeling (sick, rested, stressed . . .)? After you complete your meditation, jot down how you feel. Do you feel more calm, relaxed, or centered? You may need to practice your quiet time routine a few times before you start to notice the benefits . . . and hear your inner voice.

- Keep Lifesaver Tool #32 beside you during your quiet time. Each time you "hear" a troubling thought, write a key word down. Then let that thought go. By recognizing the thought, concern, or worry, you will be able to let it go more easily. After you have enjoyed your peaceful, quiet time, you can then deal with the troubling thoughts from a place of inner calm.

"Before and After" Yoga Reflection Sheet

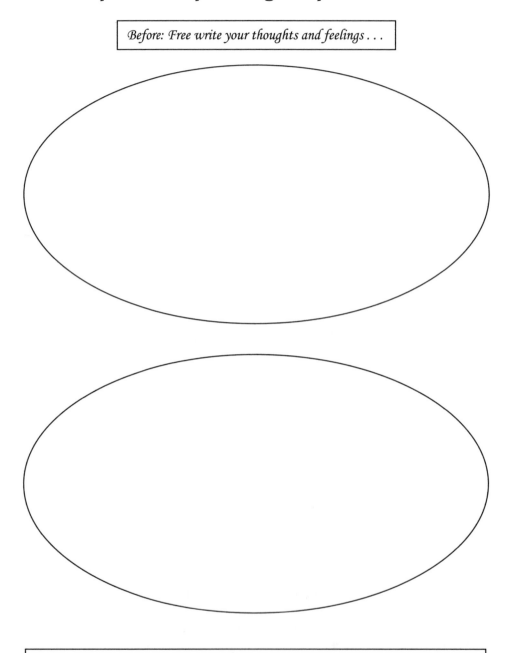

Before: *Free write your thoughts and feelings . . .*

After: *Free write your thoughts and feelings after meditation and relaxation time . . .*

Lifesaver Tool #32

Tam's To-Do

LIFESAVER #33: Think the Worst!

Pam and I are definitely opposite in how we approach problem solving! While not being a negative person, it helps me to "think the worst" in order to work mentally through the problem. As educators, we have many opportunities to become overwhelmed with worry! It has been said that stress comes from not being in control. Well, as teachers and librarians, we often feel out of control from a variety of circumstances. Use this strategy to put your problems in perspective and to relieve your worried mind!

TIPS:

- Use Lifesaver Tool #33 to work through the problem-solving model. Begin by clearly stating the problem. Next, simply picture in your mind the "worst-case scenario" and list it on the chart. Continue this process by solving each problem as if the worst had happened. By the end of the process, you know what actions you need to take to put yourself back in control.

- Consider taking a walk or a jog before and after completing Lifesaver Tool #33. Often just taking a break will give you a new perspective on the issue.

- Remember that most of our "worries" are unfounded and we can use the "cancel/cancel" strategy to stop our thoughts midstream. Next time you're thinking a worrisome thought, stop immediately and say "Cancel! Cancel!" aloud (or to yourself if you're in a crowd of people). Next, think of something—anything—else to get your mind off of the worry. Try it and you'll see that you really can change your perspective by "changing your mind."

- Share your completed tool with a friend or coworker to gain his or her insight with regards to your concerns.

- After completing the tool, ask for a meeting with your administrator or department chair if you determine your work-related concerns are valid. Ask him/her for their support in helping you reach a solution.

- Don't be afraid to ask for support. We aren't perfect—even though we try our best to be!

Think the Worst!

State the Problem:

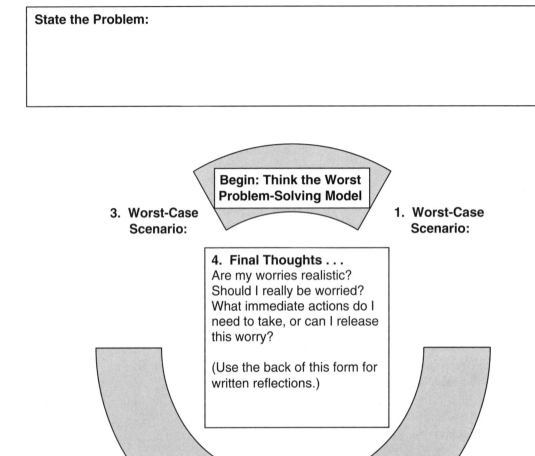

Begin: Think the Worst
Problem-Solving Model

3. Worst-Case
Scenario:

1. Worst-Case
Scenario:

4. Final Thoughts . . .
Are my worries realistic?
Should I really be worried?
What immediate actions do I
need to take, or can I release
this worry?

(Use the back of this form for
written reflections.)

2. Worst-Case
Scenario:

Lifesaver Tool #33

Pam's To-Do

LIFESAVER #34: Think the Best!

As you know, in spite of the fact that we are identical twins, we are actually very different. This lifesaver is just another example. Tam often has to catastrophize everything in order to gain a realistic perspective. I, on the other hand, refuse to consider anything but a positive solution to a problem. As I bustle around the library with a smile on my face, students often ask me, "Don't you ever get in a bad mood?" I assure them that of course I do. It's just my belief that the more positive you are, the more positive things are likely to turn out. Even when I find myself "faking" a positive mood on the outside (like when I'm not feeling well), I eventually turn positive on the inside by warding off negativity.

TIPS:

- Don't make a habit out of constantly faking a positive mental attitude. While being positive is important, it's also important to stay in touch with your inner feelings. Believe it or not, when Tam and I were in our teens, we weren't allowed to say the word "depressed" or even act depressed around my father (he couldn't deal with our teenage mood swings and drama). It took years as a grown-up to learn how I really felt on the inside. I'm happy to say that I do usually feel very positive, but I'm also quick to acknowledge (and deal with) negativity as well.

- Feeling negative? Try exercising! Take a long walk or a brisk jog. I bet you'll find you have a mood swing when you have an arm swing!

- To get feeling positive, glance through a photo album. Just by focusing on your blessings, positive memories, or cherished moments, you'll start feeling more joyful.

- Laugh! It's impossible to laugh and feel negative at the same time. Google your favorite comic strip or take a second to actually read that funny (but dumb) forward that you would normally delete.

- When you're feeling positive, take a moment to reflect and free write (use Lifesaver Tool #34). When you're feeling down, you can flip back and remember the positive times.

- Lifesaver Tools #34.2 and #34.3 are literally "tried and true!" Principal Janice True provides two positive examples in this chapter's Tried Its!

Think the Best!

Lifesaver Tool #34.1

Think the Best! (Example)

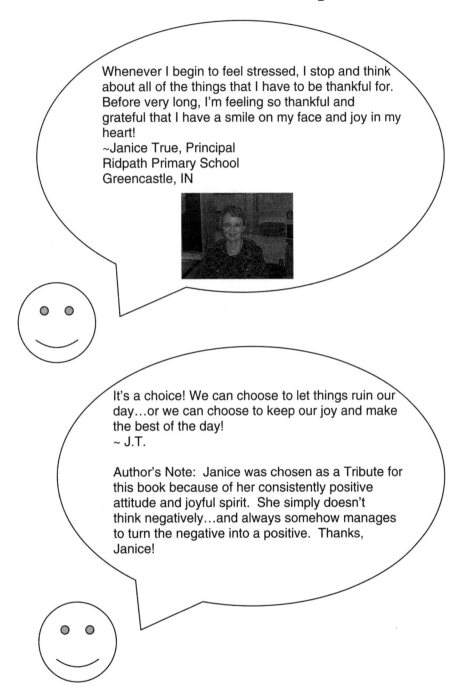

Whenever I begin to feel stressed, I stop and think about all of the things that I have to be thankful for. Before very long, I'm feeling so thankful and grateful that I have a smile on my face and joy in my heart!
~Janice True, Principal
Ridpath Primary School
Greencastle, IN

It's a choice! We can choose to let things ruin our day…or we can choose to keep our joy and make the best of the day!
~ J.T.

Author's Note: Janice was chosen as a Tribute for this book because of her consistently positive attitude and joyful spirit. She simply doesn't think negatively…and always somehow manages to turn the negative into a positive. Thanks, Janice!

Lifesaver Tool #34.2

From *Library Lifesavers: A Survival Guide for Stressed Out Librarians* by Pamela S. Bacon and Tamora K. Bacon. Santa Barbara, CA: Libraries Unlimited. Copyright © 2010.

Our To-Do

LIFESAVER #35: Move It All Week . . . Then Rest It All Weekend!

Too many times with stressful jobs, we pack everything into the weekend . . . just to become more tired when the next week starts. Because we're so busy at work during the week, we decide to exercise more on the weekend to make up for it. Then, of course, there's the grocery shopping, house cleaning, kid shuttle, let alone any kind of a social life (yawn). This lifesaver lets you plan your exercise time and your rest time. You can "move it" during the week and "rest it" all weekend . . . or plan for equal parts of exercise and rest during the weekend. The choice "rests" with you!

TIPS:

- Use Lifesaver Tool #35.1 to plan out and/or record your exercise routine for the week. By scheduling your exercise routine in advance, you may find you're more likely to stick to it and "move" ahead with your goals.

- Use Lifesaver Tool #35.2 to plan your opportunities for resting your mind. Remember: Power napping is like yoga for your mind!

- You may also use Lifesaver Tool #35.2 to plan a much-needed "weekend in bed" retreat. You may feel guilty when you plan your first weekend retreat. Remember, you deserve it. You can't meet anyone else's needs until you've rested and met your own.

- Don't beat yourself up if you find you don't meet your goals . . . give it a rest and try, try again.

- Read *Change Your Life Without Getting Out of Bed* by SARK.

- Keep Lifesaver Tools #35.1 and 35.2 for future reflections. Where did you do your best? How could you improve for the "rest" of your week and/or future weeks?

Make It Work . . . Out!

Weekly Planner		
Date/Time Scheduled:	Activity:	Did It!
Monday:		Y N
Tuesday:		Y N
Wednesday:		Y N
Thursday:		Y N
Friday:		Y N
Saturday:		Y N
Sunday:		Y N
Comments/reflections/changes to be made:		

Lifesaver Tool #35.1

Rest Your Mind . . . and Body!

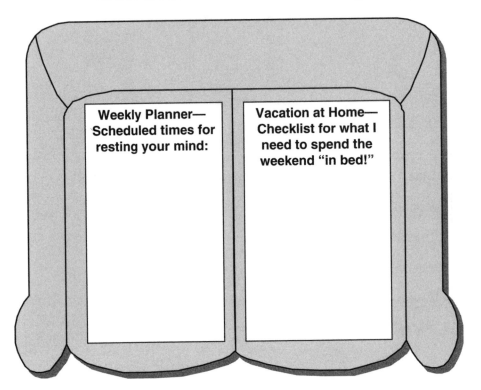

Weekly Planner— Scheduled times for resting your mind:

Vacation at Home— Checklist for what I need to spend the weekend "in bed!"

Lifesaver Tool #35.2

TALK ABOUT IT: COUNSELOR'S CORNER

While I have always been a huge fan of physical exercise (literally also since my husband is a high school basketball coach!), I also recommend meditation. Some people mistakenly confuse meditation with hypnosis. Remember that meditation is an active mental process, not passive. Your goal is to actively eliminate outside thoughts in order to completely relax your mind and body. I encourage you to try it for twenty to thirty minutes. It really helps me to feel more centered—especially before a big game!

Hey, Pam . . . wake up! Can you believe we've finished the final chapter? Let's dance!

Tam

I was just meditating! After all, we have worked our mind and body pretty hard in this chapter. The "rest" is up to our readers!

Pam

Think and Reflect: Journal Prompt

They say life is a series of routines and patterns that we create for ourselves. Commit to taking the necessary steps to exercise your mind and body in a healthy way.

Take some time to positively visualize yourself as you want to look and feel! Be specific. What are you wearing? What are you doing? Who is with you? How do you feel? You **can** make your vision a reality!

Sailing off to new adventures are Pam (in front, of course!) and Tam (the controller), the Self-Help Sisters! We hope you set sail on a new adventure soon with survival strategies and renewing activities to anchor you! Happy sailing!

_____

_____

_____

_____

_____

_____

_____

_____

_____

_____

_____

_____

_____

_____

_____

_____

_____

_____

_____

_____

_____

_____

_____

_____

_____

_____

_____

_____

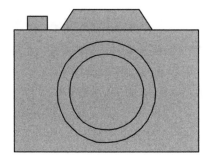

Take a Trip!

T-Take Action

http://www.motivational-messages.com/goals.html

Tam's Top Trip: I have always loved reading motivational self-help books! Here is a trip entitled just that! If you need encouragement along with specific steps for goal setting, this is for you.

http://www.shambles.net/pages/school/librarians/

Pam's Pick: This link literally takes you on a trip "around the world" to see what is current in libraries elsewhere. I especially enjoyed reading about the changing roles of the librarians. You can travel there without even packing a bag!

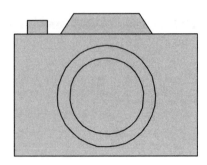

Take a Trip!

H-Hurry No More Time Management

http://www.time-management-guide.com/plan.html

Tam's Top Trip: This site includes action planning steps with recommendations for handling stress, burnout, and even some recommended audiotapes for motivation!

http://www.mindtools.com/pages/article/newTCS_01.htm

Pam's Pick: There is no need to go out of your "mind!" This trip has directions for creating a stress diary as well as other links to tools for giving you back your peace of mind!

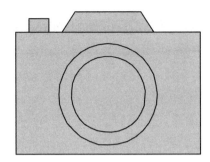

Take a Trip!

R-Read and Renew

http://www.betterworldbooks.com

Tam's Top Trip: Not only does this company offer personal customer service that is so often lost in today's busy world, but a portion of their proceeds go to global literacy efforts and environmental issues. Don't be surprised to receive a personal response, as well as a friendly thank-you note written by your book (how fun . . . see example below).

> *"Hello, Tamora! Your book asked me to write a personal note—*
> *it seemed unusual, but who are we to say no?) Holy Canasta! It's*
> *me . . . it's me! I can't believe it is actually me! You could have picked*
> *any of more than 2 million books but you picked me! I've got to get*
> *packed! How is the weather where you live? Will I need a dust*
> *jacket? I can't believe I'm leaving Mishawaka, Indiana, already—*
> *the friendly people, the Hummer plant, the Linebacker Lounge—*
> *so many memories. I don't have much time to say goodbye to*
> *everyone, but it's time to see the world!*
> *I can't wait to meet you! You sound like such a well-read person.*
> *Although, I have to say, it sure has taken you a while! I don't mean*
> *to sound ungrateful, but how would you like to spend five months*
> *sandwiched between Jane Eyre (drama queen) . . .*
> *I know the trip to meet you will be long and fraught with peril,*
> *but after the close calls I've had, I'm ready for anything*
> *(besides, some of my close friends are suspense novels). . . ."*

Be sure to order soon from this good-humored, customer-savvy book company so you can see how YOUR book's story ends!

http://www.ideamarketers.com/?Avoiding_Self_Sabotage&articleid=454894

Pam's Pick: What is your "reading style" for self-help? This site includes a variety of resources from audiotape recommendations to articles and books. I always drive Tam crazy with my personal pick of audiotapes with British accents, but to each his/her own!

P.S.: Take a moment to read the article about self-sabotage and the importance of believing in yourself—a key factor in renewal and moving forward in achieving your dreams.

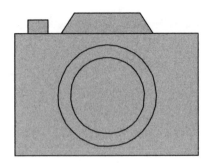

Take a Trip!

I-Inspire and Invigorate

http://www.howmuchjoy.com/links.html

Tam's Top Trip: How much joy can you handle? This site includes an abundance of inspirational links and self-help tips for creating a more balanced and joyful life. As a working mother, I especially enjoyed http://www.bluesuitmom.com for my constant goal of seeking balance!

http://www.heartsandminds.org/quotes/quotes.htm#Quotes

Pam's Pick: I have always been told that I have a heart for helping others . . . this site provides inspirational quotes to motivate and inspire you, as well as help you reach out to others!

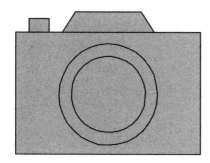

Take a Trip!

V-Vision

http://www.self-improvement-to-personal-development.com/visualization-techniques.html

Tam's Top Trip: Strategies for positive visualization can be found on this Web site—"view" it soon!

http://www.sonic.net/~erisw/bdlib.html

Pam's Pick: Do others view librarians as stuffy or traditional? Check out this site to see how the belly dancing librarian changes the stereotypical view—if you can "stomach" it!

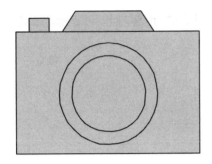

Take a Trip!

E-Exercise Your Mind and Body

http://www.mamashealth.com/exercise/mindbody.asp

Tam's Top Trip: Do you find that you continue to put yourself at the bottom of your priority list? This trip helps you see the need to prioritize your needs for exercising your mind and body! "Work it out!"

http://www.aboutaerobics.com/mind-body-exercise.html

Pam's Pick: Although I'm a yoga fan, this trip goes through a variety of options for you to select what type of exercise works best for you. Of course, I especially enjoyed the link on what to wear . . . always the fashionista—even in the gym!

Bibliography

Bianco, Arnie. *One-Minute Discipline: Classroom Management Strategies That Work.* San Francisco: Jossey-Bass, 2002.

Blanchard, Kenneth. *The One-Minute Manager Meets the Monkey.* New York: William Morrow, 1991.

Byrne, Rhonda. *The Secret.* Hillsboro, OR: Atria Books/Beyond Words, 2006.

Canfield, Jack. *Key to Living the Law of Attraction: A Simple Guide to Creating the Life of Your Dreams.* Deerfield Beach, FL: Health Communications, 2007.

Curwin, Richard, and Mendler, Allen. *Discipline with Dignity.* New York: Prentice-Hall, 2001.

Esquith, Rafe. *Teach Like Your Hair's on Fire: The Methods and Madness Inside Room 56.* New York: Penguin Books, 2007.

Hay, Louise. *You Can Heal Your Life.* Carlsbad, CA: Hay House, 2007.

Jones, Fredric. *Fred Jones Tools for Teaching: Discipline, Instruction, and Motivation.* Santa Cruz, CA: Fredric H. Jones & Associates, 2007.

McGee-Cooper, Ann. *Time Management for Unmanageable People: The Guilt-Free Way to Organize, Energize, and Maximize Your Life.* New York: Bantam Books, 1994.

McGee-Cooper, Ann. *You Don't Have to Go Home from Work Exhausted!* New York: Bantam Books, 1989.

Morgenstern, Julie. *Organizing from the Inside Out, second edition: The Foolproof System for Organizing Your Home, Your Office, and Your Life.* New York: Henry Holt, 2004.

Richardson, Cheryl. *Take Time for Your Life: A Personal Coach's 7-step Program for Creating the Life You Want.* New York: Broadway Books, 1999.

Rubinstein, Gary. *Reluctant Disciplinarian: Advice on Classroom Management from a Softy Who Became (Eventually) a Successful Teacher.* Fort Collins, CO: Cottonwood Press, 1999.

SARK. *Change Your Life without Getting Out of Bed: The Ultimate Nap Book.* New York: Fireside Books, 1999.

Thompson, Julia. *Discipline Survival Kit for the Secondary Teacher.* San Francisco: Jossey-Bass, 1998.

Tolle, Eckhart. *A New Earth: Awakening to Your Life's Purpose.* New York: Plume, 2008.

Index

ABOUT THE AUTHORS
(a.k.a. The Self-Help Sisters)

PAMELA S. BACON has spent eighteen years in education—the majority of that time working as a library media director. To have more time to read, she snuck out of the media center and is now the reading coordinator for her school. She has written many articles for teenagers and published several professional books for Libraries Unlimited.

TAMORA K. BACON has spent twenty years in the trenches. She is now thriving as her school's literacy coordinator—after surviving several years as an administrator (don't hold that against her!).

CONTRIBUTORS

Becky Greenlee, counselor, Greencastle School Corporation (Greencastle, Indiana).

Janice True, principal, Ridpath Primary School (Greencastle, Indiana).

Amy Weliever, media specialist, Greencastle Middle School (Greencastle, Indiana).

Nancy Witty, media specialist, Rockville Elementary School (Rockville, Indiana).